instant
Japanese

a pocketful of useful phrases

by
Masahiro Watanabe
and
Kei Nagashima

YOHAN PUBLICATIONS, INC.

COPYRIGHT ©1964

1st Printing	April	1964	30th Printing	February	1980
2nd Printing	June	1964	31st Printing	March	1981
3rd Printing	August	1964	32nd Printing	May	1982
4th Printing	September	1964	33rd Printing	May	1983
5th Printing	October	1964	34th Printing	February	1984
6th Printing	November	1965	35th Printing	December	1984
7th Printing	May	1966	36th Printing	July	1985
8th Printing	September	1966	37th Printing	October	1986
9th Printing	February	1967	38th Printing	February	1988
10th Printing	June	1967	39th Printing	January	1990
11th Printing	November	1967	40th Printing	July	1991
12th Printing	April	1968	41st Printing	November	1992
13th Printing	July	1968	42nd Printing	January	1994
14th Printing	December	1968	43rd Printing	December	1994
15th Printing	May	1969	(Revised Edition)		
16th Printing	August	1969	44th Printing	July	1996
17th Printing	November	1969	45th Printing	September	1997
18th Printing	February	1970	46th Printing	December	1998
19th Printing	March	1970			
(Revised Edition)					
20th Printing	April	1971			
21st Printing	November	1971			
22nd Printing	May	1972			
23rd Printing	October	1972			
24th Printing	March	1973			
25th Printing	September	1973			
26th Printing	May	1975			
27th Printing	July	1976			
28th Printing	February	1977			
29th Printing	December	1978			

Library of Congress Catalog Card No. 63-22539

YOHAN PUBLICATIONS, INC.
14-9 Okubo 3-chome, Shinjuku-ku, Tokyo, Japan

Printed in Japan

CONTENTS

CONTENTS

FOREWORD

More and more travelers are coming to Japan every year. Large ultra-modern hotels have mushroomed all over Japan to accomodate the thousands of tourists pouring in from all corners of the earth. The tourist seasons, formerly limited to spring and autumn, now continue all year round. The foreigners coming to Japan are no longer just the adventurous explorers of what some still consider the "mysterious" Orient; nowadays a good number of them are businessmen who come to our country to do business. The ancient land of *geisha* girls, the cherry blossoms and Mt. Fuji has since developed into one of the leading industrial nations in the world. It is certain that tourists these days do not leave Japan with just pearls, lacquer ware and silks. Cameras, radios and watches, all rated among the world's best, are all very important items on everyone's shopping lists as well.

Unlike Europe, where the English-speaking tourist is not too badly off, the tourist in Japan faces a significant language barrier. Although many Japanese have recognized the importance of mastering English, there are still many who cannot speak at all. And as far as native English speakers and Europeans are concerned, I imagine Japanese to be a substaintially greater task to learn than say "Greek" or "Spanish" that being the non-existence of similarities between Japanese and European languages.

I remember when I went abroad many years ago to visit the United States and Europe, my grasp of languages consisted of a mere handful of expressions from each country I visited. Before entering each new country I made a point of learning by heart, for example, their expressions for "Good morning," "How are you?" "Thank you," "How much is this?" "What fine weather it is today!" etc. Knowing these stock phrases made my travels much more enjoyable.

You have no idea how gratified I was

whenever the face of a person I spoke to lit up in surprised recognition, followed by a big smile of appreciation. It was at that time that I conceived the idea of writing some kind of book that would help tourists visiting Japan to experience the same kind of gratification that I had experienced in my travels abroad. After returning to Japan, I discussed the idea with Kei Nagashima, a friend of mine for 20 years who has since passed away. Kei was a cosmopolitan. His work involved building up better international relations at all levels and he was constantly meeting and working with people from all parts of the globe. He had also felt the need for a book of this genre to be written and so he promptly agreed to join me in this venture. Neither of us were language professors; we were two young executives—practical, but not without ideals. We shared, for instance, the belief that international goodwill and friendship on the individual level are just as important as amicable diplomatic relations at the governmental level. We wrote this little book in this spirit. It is a collection of, shall we say, many small keys that will help you to open doors of friendship and goodwill during your stay in Japan.

As we said earlier, there are many Japanese who speak some English. But, even then, any Japanese who hears you say a few words in his or her own language will be pleasantly surprised and will of course appreciate the friendly gesture. Strangely enough, the one who will get the biggest kick out of it all will be you.

"INSTANT JAPANESE" REVISED EDITION

It was just before the 1964 Tokyo Olympic Games when Kei and I first wrote this little book, and then we certainly never expected that it would become one of the best-selling books of its kind in Japan. It has been so popular that it has been necessary to revise the original edition twice, this being the latest update. Kei and I had thought that most of the how-to-learn Japanese books were too serious and dry for the short-term visitor to Japan so we decided to publish something that wouldn't be too taxing and that would also help to make your stay here as enjoyable as possible. I am extremely happy that so many friends from other countries have bought and used INSTANT JAPANESE.

Since first publishing this book vast changes have come about in Japan, and I might add, in its authors. The Japan that we described in the original edition is a completely different Japan today. For example, when we wrote the first edition we said that there were "no roads in Japan, only roads to be." Of course that is not the situation now; there are innumerable roads and highways linking all of Japan's cities, whether they be huge booming industrial cities or quiet mountain retreats, making nearly every corner of this beautiful country accessible.

I dedicate this book to my deeply missed friend, **Kei Nagashima,** who devoted most of his life to trying to better the understanding between his own people and our friends from abroad and, without whose efforts this book would never have seen the light of day. I hope that he would have agreed that this revised edition is in keeping with our original intention to improve international relations on all levels.

The illustrations have not been altered a great deal (some things are timeless!) and are a contribution by my son who was 16 years old at the time. He is now a fully-fledged businessman after having graduated from Tokyo University and having taken over my position as President of YOHAN.

I hope you will enjoy our little book and find that it is of great assistance to you while you're in Japan.

The words and phrases collected in this volume are simple, short and limited in number but selected and arranged for quick, easy and effective application. Hence our title:

"INSTANT JAPANESE . . . . . . A Pocketful of Useful Phrases."

Masahiro Watanabe

THE JAPANESE LANGUAGE
(NI-HON GO)

—a short introduction to a unique language—

1. Why Japanese is so Unique

There are no languages in the world that bear any resemblance to the Japanese language. That is perhaps why Japanese seems so unique to you. Japanese was just a spoken language until Buddhism came to Japan by way of China. Chinese characters were brought into Japan in the form of Buddhist sutras (writings) and applied to the Japanese words. That was way back in the eighth century. The oldest existing written records in Japan are dated 712 and 713 A.D.

Ever since, we have been using many Chinese characters in our writing. Japanese resembles Chinese in writing only, however. The Japanese way of reading these adopted characters is entirely different from the way that the Chinese read theirs.

2. Tokyo Dialect— Standard Japanese

There are many dialects in Japan, but the entire nation can speak what is referred to as standard Japanese which is taught at school. This is the Japanese spoken by Tokyoites. All official documents, textbooks, novels, newspapers, magazines, radio, and television use this standard Japanese. Some of the provincial dialects differ so greatly from each other that a person from the northern part of the main island of *Honshū* cannot make head or tail of what his or her fellow countrymen from the southern part of the southernmost island of *Kyūshū* are saying. However, if they were to get together, they would probably converse in standard Japanese and they'd make themselves understood. For these reasons, all of the Japanese used in this book is the official standard Japanese. Please rest assured that you will be learning only the "best" Japanese.

3. Features of the Japanese Language

a. ACCENTS ARE EXCEPTIONAL

As a rule, Japanese words are pronounced without any accent. Take, for instance, the word *"Tokyo."* Most foreigners say *"Tókyo."* Or *Yokohama* or *Osaka* for example. You would probably say *"Yokoháma"* and *"Osáka."* Unfortunately none of these pronunciations are correct. All these words should be pronounced without any accent at all. The best way to overcome the "Occidental Habit" of accentuating words is to pronounce each syllable in a Japanese word separately, like *"TŌ-KYŌ,"* *"YO-KO-HA-MA,"* and *"Ō-SA-KA,"* placing equal stress on each syllable.

b. WE HAVE NO "L"S, "TH"S OR "V"S

1. Generally the "l"s in English are pronounced as "r"s by the Japanese.

Actually the "r" in Japanese pronunciation is a fine blend of "r," "l," and "d." As a result, the Japanese people get their "l"s and "r"s all mixed up when they speak English. London becomes Rondon, "I love you" becomes "I rub you." A little Japanese stewardess may surprise you by making the announcement, "I hope you enjoy our fright," or someone may tell you that in Japan "Lice is sold on the flee market" for "rice is sold on the free market." However, we would like you to know that we are all trying to help you to enjoy your stay in Japan by speaking your language the best we can. So, please be tolerant.

2. All "th"s are pronounced like "s," "sh," "j," or "z."

The average Japanese will say to you, "I sink so" or "shink so" instead of "I think so," and

17

"Sunk you" instead of "Thank you." "This" becomes "jis," and "that" becomes "zat."

We do not wish to confuse you, but we feel it is our duty to tell you that we just don't have the "th" sound in our language.

3. "V"s are frequently pronounced like "b."

The very inept may say to you "Sunk you belly much" instead of "Thank you very much." This, however, is an extreme example.

c. YES AND NO

Please remember always to ask your questions in the affirmative form when you are talking to your Japanese friends. Let us explain why we advise you to do this. Supposing you did use the negative form in a simple question like "Don't you drink?" and your Japanese friend answered "Yes." You would automatically assume that he liked to drink. You would get him a glass, but when you were about to pour him one, he would

wildly wave his hands and say "No! No! No!"
Now you would be totally confused. Why didn't
he say "No" when you first asked him? Actually, your friend had informed you that he was a
teetotaler, because his "Yes" happened to be an
abbreviation of "Yes, (your question is correct),
I don't drink!"

So to make life simple, keep your questions
straight, e.g.

"Do you drink?"

"Do you smoke?"

Then, whatever answer you may get can be
taken at face value.

By the way, "*Hai*" (as in "Shanghai") is the
Japanese for "Yes." "*I-i-ye*" (*ee-ee-ye*) is "No."

d. YOU CAN OMIT PERSONAL PRONOUNS

Personal pronouns (I, you, he, she, it, we, you,
and they) are often omitted in Japanese, because

they can be inferred from the context. We are presuming that you are not going to settle down in Japan, so we advise you to be bold. We wish to teach you the most simplified form of an otherwise complicated language. Let's take an example of simplification:

I like *su-ki-ya-ki*.

(1) *Wa-ta-ku-shi wa su-ki-ya-ki ga su-ki de-su.*
     (I)   (*sukiyaki*)   (like)
    (Complete without any eliminations.)

(2) *Wa-ta-ku-shi su-ki-ya-ki su-ki-de-su.*
     (I)   (*sukiyaki*)   (like)
    (postpositions—particles suffixed to nouns to indicate their case—omitted. Still acceptable.)

(3) *Su-ki-ya-ki su-ki-de-su.*
    (*sukiyaki*)   (like)
    (Pronoun is omitted. Still fine.)

They are all correct. Let us make it even easier for you. Most of you know the famous Japanese dish "*Sukiyaki*" anyway. So, all you have to learn is the word "*sukidesu*" which means "like" or "fond of." The personal pronoun can be omitted, so just say,

"*Su-ki-ya-ki su-ki-de-su.*"

EXERCISE

Nip-pon su-ki-de-su. (Japan)	I like Japan.
Fuji-san su-ki-de-su. (Mt. Fuji)	I like Mt. Fuji.
Sa-ku-ra su-ki-de-su. (Cherry blossoms)	I like the cherry blossoms.
Tō-kyō su-ki-de-su.	I like Tokyo.
Kyō-to su-ki-de-su.	I like Kyoto.
Su-mi-e su-ki-de-su. (Japanese monochrome paintings)	I like *su-mi-e*.

Sa-ke su-ki-de-su.   I like *sa-ke*.
(Japanese rice wine)

Ta-ba-ko su-ki-de-su.   I like cigarettes.
(Cigarettes)

A-na-ta su-ki-de-su.   I like you.
(You)

In English you would say, "Here is a flower" or "Here are flowers" depending on how many flowers you are talking about. In Japanese we would say "*Hana ga arimasu*" whether there are thousands of flowers or just one.

4. Japanese Pronunciation

a. VOWELS ARE PRONOUNCED AS IN LATIN

There are only the five basic vowels, and these are pronounced exactly as the vowels in Latin.

When pronounced short:

    a —like the "u" in but and cut
    i —like the "i" in pin and ink
    u —like the "u" in put and full
    e —like the "e" in end and egg
    o —like the "o" in stop and fog

When pronounced long:

    ā —like the "ar" in park and farm
    i-i —like the "ee" in peel and feet
    ū —like the "oo" in pool and fool
    ē —like the "a" in pale and fate
    ō —like the "or" in port and fort

b. CONSONANTS

The consonants, *k, s, t, n, h, m, y, r, w, g, d, b, z* and *p* are pronounced as the consonants in Latin or English.

sh—like the "sh" in ship and shell
ch—like the "ch" in cherry and chimney
ts —like the "ts" in nets and parents
j —like the "dge" in bridge and judge

c. DOUBLE CONSONANTS

Whenever you see double consonants in Japanese words, (e.g., *kk*, *pp*), remember that you actually have to pronounce them like double consonants. In English, the double consonants are pronounced the same as single consonants.

The best way for you to pronounce Japanese words with double consonants correctly is to insert a 0.02-second pause between the two consonants. You don't really have to buy yourself a stopwatch. All we are suggesting is a very short pause.

Nippon	*Nip-pon*
Nikkō	*Nik-kō*
Beppu	*Bep-pu*
Hokkaidō	*Hok-kaidō*
Sapporo	*Sap-poro*

d. NO JAPANESE WORDS END IN CONSONANTS

All Japanese words end in vowels. That is the reason why all those English words ending in consonants that have been adopted into our language are pronounced with an extra vowel added to the end. For example, bed becomes "*bed-do*," desk is "*de-su-ku*," and hotel is "*ho-te-ru*." One exception is "*n*." "*N*" at the end of a word is pronounced like the "n" in the English words "ping-pong," "ding-dong," or "Hong Kong."

e. KANA

In writing, we do not use the European alphabet but instead we use two groups of syllabaries called *KANA*, which are perhaps the closest equivalent to your alphabet. They are called *KA-TA-KA-NA* and *HI-RA-GA-NA*.

All Japanese domestic cables are written and sent in *KA-TA-KA-NA*.

All foreign words are written with *KA-TA-KA-NA*.

For example:

Lincoln	リンカーン	hotel	ホテル
Washington	ワシントン	taxi	タクシー
computer	コンピュータ	coffee	コーヒー

26

THE *KA-TA-KA-NA* SYLLABARY

(formed in the 8th Century)

	A ア	I イ	U ウ	E エ	O オ
K	KA カ	KI キ	KU ク	KE ケ	KO コ
S	SA サ	SHI シ	SU ス	SE セ	SO ソ
T	TA タ	CHI チ	TSU ツ	TE テ	TO ト
N	NA ナ	NI ニ	NU ヌ	NE ネ	NO ノ
H	HA ハ	HI ヒ	FU フ	HE ヘ	HO ホ
M	MA マ	MI ミ	MU ム	ME メ	MO モ
Y	YA ヤ	I イ	YU ユ	E エ	YO ヨ
R	RA ラ	RI リ	RU ル	RE レ	RO ロ
W	WA ワ	I ヰ	U ウ	E ヱ	WO ヲ
	-NG ン				

SONANT & HALF-SONANT SYLLABLES

	A ア	I イ	U ウ	E エ	O オ
G	GA ガ	GI ギ	GU グ	GE ゲ	GO ゴ
Z	ZA ザ	JI ジ	ZU ズ	ZE ゼ	ZO ゾ
D	DA ダ			DE デ	DO ド
B	BA バ	BI ビ	BU ブ	BE ベ	BO ボ
P	PA パ	PI ピ	PU プ	PE ペ	PO ポ

THE *HI-RA-GA-NA*

(formed in the 9th Century)

Although we do not think it is that important for you to learn *HI-RA-GA-NA*, we must tell you a little about it. *HI-RA-GA-NA* was introduced by the great Buddhist Saint, *KŌ-BŌ DA-I-SHI*, in the 9th Century. The amazing thing about him was that this man was able to arrange the whole set of 48 syllables in a beautiful poetic verse called "*I-RO-HA*," without using a single syllable twice! Here it is:

I RO HA NI HO HE TO
いろはにほへと
CHI RI NU RU WO
ちりぬるを
WA KA YO TA RE SO
わかよたれそ
TSU NE NA RA MU
つねならむ
U WI NO O KU YA MA
うゐのおくやま

KE FU KO E TE
けふこえて

A SA KI YU ME MI SHI
あさきゆめみし

WE HI MO SE SU UN
ゑひもせすん

The traditional translation of this poem is as follows:

"All is transitory in this fleeting world. Let me escape from its illusions and vanities."

JAPAN
(NIP-PON)

—A short revision of what you
may already know—
"Yō-ko-so" (We're so glad you have come!)

MONTANA

Now that you have arrived in this picturesque little island nation of ours, we want you to come out and meet its friendly, hardworking people, to witness and participate in its old traditions and modern ways of life, and enjoy the beauty of its countryside to your heart's content.

1. General Background

Japan consists of four main islands and over 500 small islets. The four main islands from north to south are;

HOK-KA-I-DŌ,   HON-SHŪ,   SHI-KO-KU, and *KYŪ-SHŪ.*

The size of Japan (145,000 sq. miles) is a little less than 4% of the United States. She is actually smaller than the State of Montana (147,000 sq. miles).

The population, however, is about 50% of the United States. Only 16% of the land is arable. If you take, for example, an island about the size of the State of Montana, make only one-sixth of the land suitable for cultivation, and put half of the population of the United States onto it, you would have a pretty good idea of the basic economic problem of Japan—TOO MANY PEOPLE and TOO LITTLE LAND.

Japan must work hard for the survival of her 123,000,000 people and export as much as she possibly can. Since the war, Japan has been placing particular emphasis on the quality of her exportable products, and now many products "Made in Japan" are rated among the best in the world.

Total Area:	145,670 sq. miles (Montana 147,138 sq. miles)
Population:	123,000,000

Climate:

Spring　(Mar. Apr. May): mild

Summer (June, July, Aug.): hot
　　(June—rainy season—muggy)

Autumn　(Sep. Oct. Nov.): mild
　　(Sep.—typhoon season—stormy)

Winter　(Dec. Jan. Feb.): cold
　　(Don't forget to take your thick woolen socks along on visits to temples, Japanese inns, restaurants, and homes, where you will be asked to remove your shoes before entering.)

2. Transportation

Always-on-the-dot railway services crisscross the entire country. Swift domestic airline services connect the main cities with numerous flights every day. Taxis are reliable and charge by the meter. For longer distances larger limousines can be chartered by the day from around ¥60,000.

We recommend that you take a ride on the New *Tōkaidō/Sanyō Shinkansen* Line (Bullet train) that now runs between Tokyo and *Fukuoka (Hakata)* via Kyoto and Osaka in about five hours. This is now one of the fastest and most comfortable trains in the world, averaging a speed of 270 km/h. If, however, you are planning to travel to the northeast part of *Honshū*, the *Tōhoku-Yamagata Shinkansen* Line (Tokyo-*Morioka/Yamagata*) and the *Jōetsu Shinkansen* Line (Tokyo-*Niigata*) service this area well. Both lines began operating in 1982. Two buffet cars are attached to all of the above-mentioned trains and serve light meals and drinks.

3. Accommodations

There are many fine Western-style hotels in all major cities and resort areas throughout Japan. Don't forget that "confirmed reservations" are a must, especially during the tourist seasons of Spring and Autumn.

May we make one suggestion at this point? Try to stay at least one night in a Japanese inn, and really participate in the Japanese way of living. It can be a memorable experience.

There's no need to be afraid, because there are a number of very fine Japanese inns in most cities which know how to make you feel at home. Room rates are about the same as the Western-style hotels. Just ask your travel agent to make the necessary arrangements.

4. Roads and Taxi Drivers

Japanese roads, especially in the major cities, are by no means the best in the world. However when you take into consideration the ceaseless hordes of cars, heavy trucks, taxis, etc. using them day and night, then it's no surprise.

Road construction has simply not been able to keep up with the rapid growth of traffic as cars became a more affordable and fashionable form of transport.

Where else in the world do young people often list "driving" as their hobby?

The traveler who visits Japan for the first time may be surprised to find stretches of the main streets in large cities like Tokyo and Osaka covered with steel or asphalt plates. These "steel (or asphalt) streets," however, happen to be subway construction sites and will become nicely paved again once the subways are completed.

Wherever you go, you will find people working on the roads day and night, and it is often amusing to foreigners to count just how many people are employed simply to wave the traffic along. Although all the main streets and highways are paved, many of them are also "waved" and "caved." Ponds and puddles appear on the roads after a heavy rainfall and if you're here during the rainy season in June you'll soon realize that umbrellas can be quite ineffective when the rain is coming from all directions.

The Japanese taxi driver has become world-famous for his nerve-shattering prowess on the road. He even scares the daylights out of his own countrymen, who call him "*KA-MI-KA-ZE*," the Divine Wind.

"*MOT-TO YUK-KU-RI!!*" "More slowly please!!" learn this phrase! It may be more important to you than "Good Morning" or "Thank you."

We're almost ready now to go into our Conversation Exercises. But before we do, we would like to suggest two things:

1. When you speak English to us, please do

so "*MOT-TO YUK-KU-RI!!* (More slowly)" and

2. When we speak Japanese to you, you should request that we speak "*MOT-TO YUK-KU-RI.*"

AT
THE
AIRPORT

The New Tokyo International Airport is known
to us as "*NA-RI-TA KŪKŌ*" (*Narita* Airport).
Narita is the name of the town nearest to the
airfield. It was famous as a Buddhist temple
town before flying was ever thought of. Immi-
gration, quarantine, and customs are no different
from those in any other country. Japanese customs
officials generally are quite friendly, and all speak
and understand enough English to carry out their
duties. When you find your luggage and the in-
spector comes around, just say to him in English, "I
have nothing to declare" and, "They are all personal items" and he will understand. He might ask
you to open one bag, and he will say so in English.

Don't forget, whatever you say to him in
English, please say it as *YUK-KU-RI* (slowly) as
you can. After having passed the inspection, you
will be free to leave the terminal building with your
baggage. Your "rescue squads" at the airport, in
case you run into language difficulties, are as
follows:

1. Your airline counter.

2. Japan Travel Bureau Booth.
3. The Terminal Building's Information
   Counter in the main lobby.

However, here are some words and phrases
which you can practice at the airport:

| Yes | *Ha-i* |
| No | *I-i-ye* (Pronounced *ee-ee-ye*—if the "*i*" is pronounced too quickly, it becomes "*ie*" which means "house.") |

PICKING OUT YOUR BAGGAGE

That one!	*So-re!*
and	*to*
That one and that one!	*So-re to So-re!*

Mine	*Wa-ta-ku-shi no!* (The "*u*" is silent.)
That is mine!	*So-re wa wa-ta-ku-shi no!*
Thank you very much.	*Dō-mo* (This means "Very much" and is an abbreviation of *"Dōmo arigatō gozaimasu."* You can express your gratitude amply without learning the complete phrase. Just say *"dōmo"* and look very grateful.)
Nothing to declare.	*Shin-ko-ku su-ru mo-no wa a-ri-ma-sen.*
Here is my passport.	*Ko-re ga wa-ta-ku-shi-no pa-su-pō-to de-su.*
It's all personal items.	*Zen-bu wa-ta-ku-shi no mo-chi-mo-no de-su.*

44

This is all I have.　　*Ko-re de zen-bu de-su.*

Please open it.　　*Dō-zo a-ke-te ku-da-sa-i.*

WANTING TO FIND OUT
WHAT TIME IT IS NOW IN TOKYO

Now　　*I-ma*

What time is it?　　*Nan-ji de-su ka?* (The "*u*" is not pronounced in "*de-su ka*." So this becomes "*deska*.")

What time is it now?　　*I-ma nan-ji (de-su ka)?* (Note: All questions in Japanese end with the interrogative suffix "*ka?*")

45

WANTING TO GET SOME LOCAL MONEY

bank	*gin-kō*
Where is?	*Do-ko de-su ka?*
Where is the bank?	*Gin-kō do-ko de-su ka?*
I want to change money.	*Ryō-ga-e shi-te ku-da-sai.*

CLAIMING YOUR BAGGAGE

baggage	*ni-mo-tsu*
my, mine	*wa-ta-ku-shi no*
Where is my baggage?	*Wa-ta-ku-shi no ni-mo-tsu do-ko de-su-ka?*
Get me a porter* please.	*Pō-tā-san o yon-de ku-da-sai.*
Could you please call me a taxi.	*Ta-ku-shi-i o yon-de ku-da-sai.*

Take me to ....*e it-te ku-da-sa-i.*
  please.......

* The porters at the airport wear a cream
uniform with maroon arm bands and maroon
belt. Their charge is ¥300 per average piece.
A small tip to a nice obliging fellow is always
appreciated, although not compulsory. We
usually tip the porters about ¥300 if they are
especially helpful.

LOOKING FOR A CAR TO TAKE YOU TO YOUR HOTEL

taxi	*ta-ku-shi-i*
large car for hire	*ha-i-yā*
limousine	*ri-mu-jin*
Where can I get a taxi?	*Ta-ku-shi-i do-ko de-su ka?*

FROM THE AIRPORT TO THE HOTEL

please	*o-ne-ga-i shi-ma-su*
to	*e* (short)
To the ......Hotel, please.	*......ho-te-ru e o-ne-ga-i shi-ma-su.*
Go slower please!	*Mot-to yuk-ku-ri o-ne-ga-i shi-ma-su.*
this place	*ko-ko* (both "*o*"s are very short.)
To this place, please!	*Ko-ko e o-ne-ga-i shi-ma-su.*
(Do you) understand?	*Wa-ka-ri-ma-su-ka?*
Do you know this place?	*Ko-ko wa-ka-ri-ma-su-ka?*
Stop!	*Su-top-pu! (To-me-te!)*
How much is it?	*I-ku-ra de-su ka?*
this	*ko-re*
tip	*chip-pu*
This is a tip**(for you)	*Ko-re chip-pu de-su.*
Give me ... please.	*... o ku-da-sa-i.*

| change | *o-tsu-ri* (The "*o*" is very, very, short.) |
| Keep the change. (I don't want the change.) | *O-tsu-ri wa i-ri-ma-sen.* |

** We very, very rarely tip our taxi drivers. We do so only when the driver is a friendly, cooperative fellow who has helped us with our baggage, or who has delivered us safely to our destination without shattering our nerves. About 10% of the fare, if you feel he deserves it, would be a nice gesture of gratitude.

GREETING YOUR JAPANESE FRIENDS WHO HAVE COME OUT TO WELCOME YOU

| Good morning | *O-ha-yō* |
| Good day | *Kon-ni-chi-wa* |

49

Good evening	*Kon-ban wa*
I am Mr. Smith.	*Wa-ta-ku-shi Smith de-su.*
name	*na-ma-e*
my name	*wa-ta-ku-shi no na-ma-e*
My name is Paul Smith.	*Wa-ta-ku-shi no na-ma-e Paul Smith de-su.*
you	*a-na-ta*
your	*a-na-ta no*
(What is) your name?	*A-na-ta no na-ma-e wa?*

IF YOU WANT TO CALL SOMEONE FROM THE AIRPORT

telephone	*den-wa*
Where is a telephone?	*Den-wa do-ko de-su ka?*
hotel	*ho-te-ru*

50

embassy	*ta-i-shi-kan*
consulate	*ryō-ji-kan*
company	*ka-i-sha*
my company	*wa-ta-ku-shi no ka-i-sha*
friend	*to-mo-da-chi*
my friend(s)	*wa-ta-ku-shi no to-mo-da-chi*

MOST USEFUL WORDS TO KNOW

That one!	*So-re!*
I	*wa-ta-ku-shi*
my, mine	*wa-ta-ku-shi no*
you	*a-na-ta*
your	*a-na-ta no*
Thank you very much.	*Dō-mo.* (Don't forget to look grateful when you say it.)
What time is it now?	*I-ma nan-ji de-su ka?*
Where is…?	*... do-ko de-su ka?*
Yes!	*Ha-i!*

No!	*I-i-ye* (pronounced *ee-ee ye*)
Good morning	*O-ha-yō*
Good day	*Kon-ni-chi wa*
Good evening	*Kon-ban wa*
name	*na-ma-e*
What is your name?	*A-na-ta no na-ma-e wa?*
My name is……	*Wa-ta-ku-shi no na-ma-e…… de-su.*

VOCABULARY

address	*jū-sho*
age	*nen-re-i*
airline	*kō-kū ga-i-sha*
airplane	*hi-kō-ki*
airport	*kū-kō*
ambassador	*ta-i-shi*
attendant	*a-ka-bō-san* (at railway station)

baggage	*ni-mo-tsu*
heavy	*o-mo-i*
light	*ka-ru-i*
bank	*gin-kō*
bus	*ba-su*
camera	*ka-me-ra*
cash	*gen-kin*
cigar	*ha-ma-ki*
cigarette	*ta-ba-ko*
clothes	*i-ru-i*
consulate	*ryō-ji-kan*
consulate general	*sō-ryō-ji-kan*
currency	*tsū-ka*
family name	*myō-ji*
foreign currency	*gai-ka*
customs duty	*kan-ze-i*
customs office	*ze-i-kan*
documents	*sho-ru-i*
embassy	*ta-i-shi-kan*
film	*fi-ru-mu*
gift	*o-mi-ya-ge*
hotel	*ho-te-ru*
inspect	*ken-sa*

legation	*kō-shi-kan*
letter of introduction	*shō-ka-i-jō*
limousine	*ri-mu-jin*
liquor	*sa-ke*
money	*o-ka-ne*
name	*na-ma-e*
nationality	*ko-ku-se-ki*
passport	*ryo-ken; pa-su-pō-to*
porter (at airport and hotel)	*pō-tā-san*
registration	*tō-ro-ku*
smuggle	We are not insinuating that you have anything to do with this. But, to satisfy your curiosity, the Japanese word is "*mi-tsu-yu.*"
telephone	*den-wa*
tip	*chip-pu*
traveler's cheque	*to-ra-be-rā chek-ku*
visa	*sa-shō; bi-za*
vaccination	*shu-tō*
certificate	*shō-me-i-sho*

AT
THE
HOTEL

You are now checking in at your hotel. At the front desk of any good hotel, the clerk will speak English well. However, you must forgive him or her if his or her pronunciation is not quite as good as your own. Again, don't forget to speak your English as "*yuk-ku-ri* (slowly)" as possible; it always helps to do so.

The hotels in Japan are known for their excellent and friendly service. We are sure you will enjoy your stay.

CHECKING IN

Do you have……?	*a-ri-ma-su ka?*
room(s)	*he-ya*
Do (you) have (a) room?	*He-ya a-ri-ma-su ka?*
Yes, (we) have.	*Ha-i, a-ri-ma-su.*
with a bath	*ba-su tsu-ki*
a single	*shin-gu-ru*
a double	*da-bu-ru*
reservation	*yo-ya-ku*

I have made reservations.	*Yo-ya-ku shi-ma-shi-ta.*
How much?	*I-ku-ra de-su ka?*
this	*ko-no*
room	*he-ya*
How much is this room?	*Ko-no he-ya i-ku-ra de-su ka?*
That's fine!	*I-i-de-su ne.*
That's perfect!	*Ta-i-hen kek-kō de-su.*
That's just right!	*To-te-mo i-i-de-su-ne.*
Okay!	*Ō-ke-i*
different	*chi-ga-u*
Do you have a different room?	*Chi-ga-u he-ya a-ri-ma-su ka?*
Do you have an inexpensive room?	*Ya-su-i he-ya a-ri-ma-su ka?*
Do you have a better room?	*Mot-to i-i he-ya a-ri-ma-su ka?*

57

GOING UP TO YOUR ROOM

floor	*ka-i; ga-i*
Which floor?	*Nan-ga-i?*
Which floor is it?	*Nan-ga-i de-su ka?*
1st floor	*ik-ka-i*
2nd floor	*ni-ka-i*
3rd floor	*san-ga-i*
4th floor	*yon-ka-i*
5th floor	*go-ka-i*
6th floor	*rok-ka-i*
7th floor	*na-na-ka-i*
8th floor	*ha-chi-ka-i*
9th floor	*kyū-ka-i*
10th floor	*juk-ka-i*
11th floor	*jū-ik-ka-i*
12th floor	*jū-ni-ka-i*
13th floor	*jū-san-ka-i*
20th floor	*ni-juk-ka-i*
30th floor	*san-juk-ka-i*
31st floor	*san-jū-ik-ka-i*
40th floor	*yon-juk-ka-i*
room number	*he-ya no ban-gō*

What number is it?	*Nan-ban de-su ka?*
key	*ka-gi*
my key	*wa-ta-ku-shi no ka-gi*
Where is my key?	*Wa-ta-ku-shi no ka-gi do-ko de-su ka?*
porter	*pō-tā san*
page boy	*bō-i san*
room maid	*mē-do san*

MEALS

breakfast (morning meal)	*a-sa go-han*
lunch (noon meal)	*hi-ru go-han*
dinner (evening meal)	*ban go-han*
what time?	*nan-ji*
from	*ka-ra*
up to; till	*ma-de*
When does the dining room open for breakfast (lunch, dinner)?	*A-sa (hi-ru, ban) go-han nan-ji ka-ra de-su ka?*

How late does the dining room stay open for breakfast? (lunch, dinner)

A-sa (hi-ru, ban) go-han nan-ji ma-de de-su ka?

dining room

sho-ku-dō

Where is the dining room?

Sho-ku-dō do-ko de-su ka?

grill

gu-ri-ru

room service

rū-mu sā-bi-su

bar

bā

SENDING OUT YOUR LAUNDRY

laundry (things to launder)

sen-ta-ku mo-no (sen-ta-ku: launder) (mo-no: things)

I have some laundry.

Sen-ta-ku mo-no a-ri-ma-su.

someone

da-re-ka

please

o-ne-ga-i shi-ma-su

Please someone come!

O-ne-ga-i shi-ma-su da-re-ka ki-te!

60

Come in! (please)	*Dō-zo !*
this	*ko-no*
Please press this .....for me.	*Ko-no....pu-re-su o-ne-ga-i shi-ma-su.*
Please wash this ....for me.	*Ko-no....sen-ta-ku o-ne-ga-i shi-ma-su.*
Please have this ..... dry cleaned.	*Ko-no....do-rai ku-ri-i-nin-gu o-ne-ga-i shi-ma-su.*
starch	*no-ri*
without	*na-shi*
when	*i-tsu*
by (up to)	*ma-de*
When will it be ready?	*I-tsu de-ki-ma-su ka?*

GETTING YOUR SHOES CLEANED

shoes	*ku-tsu*
polish	*mi-ga-i-te*
these (same as this)	*ko-re*
Please polish these for me.	*Ko-re mi-ga-i-te.* (We suggest you drop the word "please", and just say the phrase in a nice way.)
If possible, I'd like it done.......	*Mo-shi de-ki-re ba ...... shi-te ku-da-sa-i.*
now	*i-ma*
right away	*su-gu*
right now	*i-ma su-gu*
by (up to)	*ma-de*
by morning	*a-sa ma-de*
by noon	*hi-ru ma-de*
by evening	*ban ma-de*

ORDERING IN YOUR ROOM

(please) give me.......	.... *ku-da-sa-i!*
hot water	*o-yu*
ice water	*a-i-su uō-tā*
writing paper	*bin-sen*
envelope	*fū-tō*
overseas cable forms	*ko-ku-sa-i den-pō yō-shi*
Please clean (the room).	*Sō-ji shi-te ku-da-sa-i.*
Please clear the table.	*Sa-ge-te ku-da-sa-i.*
Guests are coming.	*O-kya-ku-sa-ma ga ki-ma-su.*

WALKING AROUND IN THE HOTEL

mail & telegrams	*yū-bin to den-pō*
mail	*yū-bin*
post office	*yū-bin kyo-ku*
Where is the post office?	*Yū-bin kyo-ku wa do-ko de-su ka?*

63

telegram, cable	*den-pō*
Any mail for me? (*lit.* Has mail come?)	*Te-ga-mi ki-te i-ma-su ka?*
Any telegrams for me? (Have telegrams come?)	*Den-pō ki-te i-ma-su ka?*
stamp	*kit-te*
(Please) give me...!	*...... ku-da-sa-i!*
Please give me (some) stamps!	*Kit-te ku-da-sa-i!*
How much does it cost to send to America?	*A-me-ri-ka ma-de i-ku-ra?*
postcards (picture postcards)	*ha-ga-ki (e-ha-ga-ki)*

OTHER FACILITIES IN THE HOTEL

| wash room (toilet) | *to-i-re* |
| cloak room | *ku-rō-ku* |

64

Japan Travel Bureau (JTB)	*Kō-tsū-kō-sha; je-i ti-i bi-i*
airlines	*kō-kū ga-i-sha*
barber shop	*to-ko-ya*
beauty parlor	*bi-yō-in*
shops	*mi-se*
drugs, medicine	*ku-su-ri*

AT THE CASHIER'S

cashier	*ka-i-ke-i*
cash	*gen-kin*
travelers' cheques	*to-ra-be-rā chek-ku*
convert money	*ryō-ga-e*
Will you please.......?	*...... shi-te-ku-da-sa-i.*
Will you please convert (this for me)?	*Ryō-ga-e shi-te-ku-da-sa-i.*
my bill	*o-kan-jō*
receipt	*u-ke-to-ri*
Please give me my bill.	*O-kan-jō shi-te ku-da-sa-i.*

Please make the bills separate.	*O-kan-jō be-tsu be-tsu ni shi-te ku-da-sa-i.*

USEFUL EXPRESSIONS

I'm going out.	*De-ka-ke-ma-su.*
I'll be back.	*Ka-e-ri-ma-su.*
I'll be back right away.	*Su-gu ka-e-ri-ma-su.*
I'm leaving.	*Shup-pa-tsu shi-ma-su.*
Please come and take my baggage down.	*Ni-mo-tsu to-ri ni ki-te ku-da-sa-i.*
Please get me a taxi.	*Ta-ku-shi-i o-ne-ga-i shi-ma-su.*
The heater is broken.	*Hi-i-tā ko-wa-re-te i-ma-su.*

VOCABULARY

air conditioning	*e-a kon*
ashtray	*ha-i-za-ra*
bar	*bā*
barber shop	*to-ko-ya*
bath	*fu-ro; ba-su*
bath towel	*ba-su ta-o-ru*
beauty parlor	*bi-yō-in*
bill	*o-kan-jō*
blanket	*mō-fu*
book	*hon*
breakfast	*a-sa go-han*
car	*ji-dō-sha*
chewing-gum	*chū-in ga-mu*
cigar	*ha-ma-ki*
cigarette	*ta-ba-ko*
foreign cigarette	*ga-i-ko-ku ta-ba-ko*
cloak room	*ku-rō-kū*
coffee	*kō-hi-i*
dining room	*sho-ku-dō*
dinner (supper)	*ban go-han*
door	*do-a*

double bed	*da-bu-ru bed-do*
drugs, medicine	*ku-su-ri*
dry cleaning	*do-ra-i ku-ri-i-nin-gu*
elevator	*e-re-bē-tā*
English language	*Ei-go*
English language magazine	*Ei-go no zas-shi*
English language newspaper	*Ei-go no shin-bun*
envelope	*fū-tō*
floor	*ka-i*
florist	*ha-na-ya*
flowers	*ha-na*
front desk	*fu-ron-to*
glass (for drinking)	*kop-pu*
green tea	*o-cha*
grill	*gu-ri-ru*
guest	*kya-ku*
heating	*dan-bō*
hello! (on the telephone)	*mo-shi mo-shi*
hot water	*o-yu*
ice	*kō-ri; a-i-su*

key	*ki-i*
laundry	*sen-ta-ku*
letter	*te-ga-mi*
lobby	*ro-bi-i*
lunch	*hi-ru go-han*
magazine	*zas-shi*
mail	*yū-bin*
manager	*shi-ha-i-nin; ma-nē-jā*
mosquito	*ka*
mosquito net	*ka-ya*
newspaper	*shin-bun*
noisy	*u-ru-sa-i*
overseas call	*ko-ku-sa-i den-wa*
page	*pē-ji san; bō-i san*
pillow	*ma-ku-ra*
please	*dō-zo; o-ne-ga-i shi-ma-su*
polish (shoes)	*mi-ga-ku*
post card	*ha-ga-ki*
post office	*yū-bin kyo-ku*
quiet	*shi-zu-ka-na*
receipt	*u-ke-to-ri*
reservation	*yo-ya-ku*

room	*he-ya*
room maid	*mē-do san*
room number	*he-ya no ban-gō*
room service	*rū-mu sā-bi-su*
shoes	*ku-tsu*
shop	*mi-se*
single bed	*shin-gu-ru bed-do*
soap	*sek-ken*
someone	*da-re-ka*
stairway	*ka-i-dan*
stamp	*kit-te*
starch	*no-ri*
telegram	*den-pō*
telephone	*den-wa*
towel	*ta-o-ru*
waiter	*u-e-i-tā*
waitress	*u-e-i-to-re-su*
washroom	*to-i-re*
water	*mi-zu*
window	*ma-do*

GENERAL
CONVERSATION

Now, assuming that you have settled down in your new environment, let us give you some of those everyday greetings that you can use all the time with any Japanese with whom you come in contact. Try these on your room maid, the elevator attendant or the waiters in the dining room and you will find that they will like you for it and they will bend over backwards to show their appreciation for your efforts.

GREETINGS

Good morning.	*O-ha-yō go-za-i-ma-su.*
Good afternoon. Good day. Hello. How do you do?	*Kon-ni-chi-wa.*
Good evening.	*Kon-ban-wa.*
Good night (sleep well).	*O-ya-su-mi na-sa-i.*

Good-bye. *Sa-yo-na-ra.*

This greeting of farewell is one of the nicest in existence. It means "If it must be so" ... "We do not wish to part, but if it must be so..." Isn't it nice?

Go-ki-gen-yō.

Very polite .... try it once with your better acquaintances and see their reaction. You are sure to impress them. Literally it means "fare ye well."

How are you? ⎫
Are you well? ⎭ *O-gen-ki de-su ka?*

Yes, I am fine. *Hai, gen-ki de-su.*

Pardon me. *Go-men na-sa-i.*

Excuse me. *Su-mi-ma-sen.*

Thank you.* *A-ri-ga-tō.* (friendly)
A-ri-ga-tō go-za-i-ma-su. (polite)

Thank you very *Dō-mo a-ri-ga-tō go-*
much.* *za-i-ma-su.* (polite)

73

* SPECIAL RECOMMENDATION:

The easiest and most popular way of saying "Thank you" is *DŌ-MO*. Just say "*DŌ-MO*" and look grateful. That's what we do all the time. It's like your "Oh, thanks."

Once upon a time, a tourist in Japan asked a friend for the Japanese word for "Thank you", and he was told that it was "*Arigatō*." The tourist could not memorize it, so his friend suggested that he should just think of the English word "Alligator." The next morning however, when the room maid brought his coffee, he said to her very proudly,"Oh, Crocodile." So be careful, word association can be confusing at times.

Don't mention it. *Dō-i-ta-shi ma-shi-te.* (You're welcome.)

This is a complicated one. The American servicemen stationed in Japan tried to memorize this one by thinking of "Don't toucha moustache!"

Yes	*Ha-i* (short)
No	*I-i-ye*
Please	*Dō-zo (o-ne-ga-i shi-ma-su)*

MEETING PEOPLE FOR THE FIRST TIME

I	*Wa-ta-ku-shi*
you	*A-na-ta*
he, she	*Ka-re* (he), *Ka-no-jo* (she)
we	*Wa-ta-ku-shi ta-chi*
you	*A-na-ta ta-chi*
they	*Ka-re ra* (all those males)
	Ka-no-jo ra (all those females)
name	*na-ma-e*
What is your name?	*A-na-ta no o-na-ma-e wa?* (Prefix "*o*" is used for politeness. "*O-namae*" would be "your honorable name.")
My name is Robert Linden.	Robert Linden *de-su*.
Who is that gentleman?	*A-no ka-ta da-re de-su ka?*

75

He is Mr. Lowry.	*Lowry-san de-su.*
Where are you from?	*Do-chi-ra ka-ra ki-ma-shi-ta-ka?*
I am from America.	*A-me-ri-ka ka-ra de-su.*
Where are you staying?	*Do-ko ni o-to-ma-ri de-su-ka?*
I am staying at the Imperial Hotel.	*Te-i-ko-ku Ho-te-ru ni i-ma-su.*
When did you arrive in Japan?	*I-tsu tsu-ki-ma-shi-ta ka?*
How long have you been in Japan?	*Nip-pon ni ki-te do-no ku-ra-i ni na-ri-ma-su ka?*
Do you understand English?	*Ei-go wa-ka-ri ma-su ka?*
Can we speak in English, please?	*Ei-go de ha-na-shi-ma-shō.*
Please say it again.	*Mō-i-chi-do it-te ku-da-sa-i.*
Please say it more slowly.	*Mot-to yuk-ku-ri it-te ku-da-sa-i.*
Do you understand?	*Wa-ka-ri ma-su ka?*

Yes, I understand.	*Ha-i, wa-ka-ri ma-su.*
No, I don't under-stand.	*I-i-ye, wa-ka-ri ma-sen.*

INTRODUCING OTHERS

May I introduce	*...... o go-shō-kai shi-ma-su*
Mr. (Mrs., Miss)....	*...... san*
my husband	*shu-jin*
my wife	*ka-na-i*
my son	*mu-su-ko*
my daughter	*mu-su-me*
my sister	*a-ne* (elder sister)
	i-mō-to (younger sister)
my brother	*a-ni* (elder brother)
	o-tō-to (younger brother)
my father	*chi-chi*
my mother	*ha-ha*
my grandfather	*so-fu*

my grandmother	*so-bo*
my uncle	*o-ji*
my aunt	*o-ba*
my friend	*(wa-ta-ku-shi no)*
	to-mo-da-chi

MEETING ACQUAINTANCES

Hello.	*Kon-ni-chi-wa.*
How are you?	*O-gen-ki de-su ka?*
I'm fine, thank you.	*Gen-ki de-su.*
How is business?	*Ke-i-ki wa dō de-su ka?* (in Tokyo)
	Mō-ka-ri-mak-ka? (in Osaka)
I'm doing fine.	*O-ka-ge-sa-ma-de.*
Please take a seat.	*Dō-zo o-ka-ke ku-da-sai.*
How about some coffee?	*Ko-hi-i i-ka-ga de-su ka?*
How about some tea?	*Kō-cha i-ka-ga de-su ka?*

I'm hungry.	*O-na-ka su-ki-ma-shi-ta.*
I'm thirsty.	*No-do ka-wa-ki-ma-shi-ta.*
I'm sleepy.	*Ne-mu-i de-su.*
I'm tired.	*Tsu-ka-re-ma-shi-ta.*
Make yourself at home.	*Dō-zo o-ra-ku ni.*
Don't trouble yourself.	*Dō-zo o-ka-ma-i na-ku.*
Sorry to trouble you.	*O-te-ka-zu ka-ke-te su-mi-ma-sen.*
Do you like…… ?	*…… su-ki de-su ka?*
Would you like……?	*…… i-ka-ga-de-su ka?*
Do you want……?	*…… i-ri-ma-su ka?*
Help yourself.	*Dō-zo go-ji-yū ni.*
To your health!	*Go-ken-kō o!*
Shall we go?	*I-ki-ma-shō ka?*
Let's go.	*I-ki-ma-shō.*
Sorry to trouble you, but...	*Su-mi-ma-sen ga ……*
Can you help me?	*Te-tsu-dat-te ku-re-ma-su ka?*

Can you do it?	*De-ki-ma-su ka?*
Could you please do me a favor?	*O-ne-ga-i ga a-ri-ma-su.*
Please!	*O-ne-ga-i!*
Gladly!	*Yo-ro-kon-de!*
Certainly!	*Mo-chi-ron!*
Of course!	*Mo-chi-ron!*
As quickly as possible.	*De-ki-ru da-ke ha-ya-ku.*
Thank you.	*Dō-mo; a-ri-ga-tō.*
Don't mention it. (You're welcome.)	*Dō-i-ta-shi-ma-shi-te.*
Pardon me.	*Go-men-na-sa-i.*
It doesn't matter.	*Ka-ma-i ma-sen.*
I'm sorry.	*Go-men-na-sa-i; su-mi-ma-sen.*
It's nothing.	*Nan-de-mo a-ri-ma-sen.*
I'm glad.	*U-re-shi-i de-su.*
Sorry to keep you waiting.	*O-ma-ta-se shi-ma-shi-ta.*
You have been very kind.	*Dō-mo go-shin-se-tsu ni.*

I'm most grateful.	*Kan-sha shi-ma-su.*
Best wishes to	*...... ni yo-ro-shi-ku.*
Let's meet again.	*Ma-ta a-i-ma-shō.*
See you later.	*Ja-a, ma-ta ne!*
A pleasant journey!	*It-te ras-shai!*

OTHER OFTEN USED EXPRESSIONS

What's the matter ?	*Dō-shi-ma-shi-ta?*
Be careful.	*Ki o tsu-ke-te ku-da-sa-i.*
A little more.	*Mō su-ko-shi.*
What's this?	*Ko-re wa nan de-su ka?*
Where is it?	*Do-ko de-su ka?*
Here it is.	*Ko-ko ni a-ri-ma-su.*
Is that so!	*Sō de-su ka!*
That's right, I agree with you.	*Sō de-su ne.*
I see.	*Wa-ka-ri-ma-shi-ta.*
perhaps	*mo-shi-ka-shi-ta-ra*

Not at all.	*I-i-ye, chit-to-mo.*
I think so.	*Sō o-mo-i ma-su.*
I don't think so.	*Sō o-mo-i ma-sen.*
You're wrong.	*So-re wa chi-ga-i-ma-su.*
You're right.	*So-no tō-ri de-su.*
It's all right.	*Da-i jō-bu de-su.*
O.K. (Okay)	*Ok-kē.*

CONGRATULATIONS

Congratulations.	*O-me-de-tō go-za-i-ma-su.*
Happy Birthday.	*O-tan-jō-bi o-me-de-tō.*
Merry Christmas.	*Me-ri-i ku-ri-su-ma-su.*
Happy New Year.	*Shin-nen o-me-de-tō.* *A-ke-ma-shi-te o-me-de-tō.*

82

EXCLAMATIONS

What a pity!	*O-shi-i de-su ne!*
Too bad!	*I-ke-ma-sen ne!*
Darn it!	*Chi-ku-shō!*
That's fine!	*So-re wa i-i de-su-ne!*
That's enough!	*Mō kek-kō de-su!*
Never mind!	*Ka-ma-i-ma-sen; i-i de-su, i-i de-su!*
You don't say so!	*Ma-sa-ka!*
Really?	*Hon-tō de-su ka?*
Nonsense!	*Ba-ka-na!*
What nerve!	*I-i do-kyō de-su!*
Cut it out!	*Ya-me na-sa-i!*
He's a pest.	*U-ru-sa-i ya-tsu da!*
That's wonderful!	*So-re wa su-ba-ra-shi-i!*
You bet!	*Mo-chi-ron!*
Good luck!	*Se-i-kō o i-no-ri ma-su!*
Ouch!	*I-ta-i!*

| Excuse me! (trying to get service) | *Su-mi-ma-sen!* |
| Oh, dear! | *O-ya, o-ya!* |

AT THE TABLE

"I-TA-DA-KI-MA-SU" & *"GO-CHI-SŌ-SA-MA"*
(I gratefully partake.)   (I am grateful to all who
made this meal pos-
sible.)

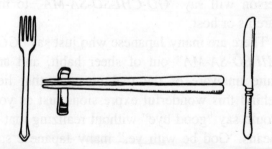

In Japan, when a child is old enough to hold his chopsticks, he is taught to say *"I-TA-DA-KI-MA-SU"* before every meal, and *"GO-CHI-SŌ-SA-MA"* after he has finished.

The expression *"I-TA-DA-KI-MA-SU"* literally means "I gratefully partake." It is not merely a salutation to one's parents, but an expression of gratitude to the gods, to nature, the animals and fish, vegetables, and to the farmers and fishermen who have made the meal possible. Whenever one is invited to tea, lunch, or dinner, he also says *"I-TA-DA-KI-MA-SU"* to his host.

When the meal is over, a polite Japanese person will say *"GO-CHI-SŌ-SA-MA"* to his parents or host.

There are many Japanese who just say *"GO-CHI-SŌ-SA-MA"* out of sheer habit, and are quite unaware of the real meaning that lies behind this wonderful expression. Just as you would say "good-bye" without realizing that it means "God be with ye," many Japanese say *"GO-CHI-SŌ-SA-MA"* in appreciation of a full stomach."*GO-CHI-SŌ-SA-MA*"literally means "Thank you for all your running around." This expression is several centuries old, and originated with the formal dinners that accompanied the ceremonial tea parties of the noblemen. It seems that the hosts at the time were so hospitable that they did a lot of "running around" to prepare for the occasion. The guests' tastes in art and nature, drinks and food were all considered of the utmost importance and so, the host would send messengers running in all directions with orders to collect certain specific objects of art, flowers, incense, wines, and delicacies which were the guests' favorites! At the end of the quiet ceremonial dinner, the guest would put all his heart into the simple expression of appreciation for all the trouble his host went to on his behalf, and say "*GO-CHI-SŌ-SA-MA* ... Thank you for your all running around.*"

So, at the beginning of a meal it is: "*I-TA-DA-KI-MA-SU*," and at the end of a meal it is: "*GO-CHI-SŌ-SA-MA*."

Try it when you are invited out for dinner by your Japanese friends. We are sure it will "unlock some doors" for you.

One way to remember "*I-TA-DA-KI-MA-SU*" is "EAT A DUCK HE MUST."

USEFUL PHRASES

invitation	*shō-ta-i*
So glad you could come.	*Yō-ko-so i-ras-sha-i ma-shi-ta.*
Thank you for inviting me.	*Go-shō-tai a-ri-ga-tō.*
How about a drink?	*Bi-i-ru i-ka-ga de-su ka?*
How about a cigarette?	*Ta-ba-ko i-ka-ga de-su ka?*
Please sit here.	*Ko-ko-ni o-su-wa-ri ku-da-sa-i.*
Are you hungry?	*O-na-ka ga su-ki ma-shi-ta ka?*
Yes, I'm hungry.	*Ha-i, O-na-ka ga su-ki ma-shi-ta.*

Are you thirsty?	*No-do ga ka-wa-ki ma-shi-ta ka?*
Yes, I'm thirsty.	*Ha-i, No-do ga ka-wa-ki ma-shi-ta.*
Let's have a drink.	*Na-ni-ka no-mi ma-shō.*
Would you like a drink?	*Na-ni-ka o-no-mi ni na-ri-ma-su ka?*
What would you like?	*Na-ni ni shi-ma-shō?*
Please show me the menu.	*Me-nyū o mi-se-te ku-da-sa-i.*

(When you are doubtful about the English-speaking ability of the waiter or the waitress, the best way to order at a restaurant in Japan is to point to the item on the menu and just say:)

I'll have this, please	*Ko-re ku-da-sa-i.*
I'll have some hors d'oeuvres, please.	*Ō-do-bu-ru ku-da-sa-i.*
I'll have soup, please.	*Sū-pu ku-da-sa-i.*
I'll have consomme, please.	*Kon-so-me ku-da-sa-i.*

89

I'll have potage, please.	*Po-tā-ju ku-da-sa-i.*
I'd like coffee, please.	*Kō-hi-i ku-da-sa-i.*
I'd like tea, please.	*Kō-cha ku-da-sa-i.*
No sugar or milk, thank you.	*O-sa-tō mo mi-ru-ku mo kek-kō de-su.*
Tea with lemon, please.	*Re-mon ti-i ku-da-sa-i.*
Give me a second helping.	*O-ka-wa-ri ku-da-sa-i.*
Please help yourself.	*Dō-zo go-ji-yū ni.*
How about some more?	*Mō su-ko-shi i-ka-ga de-su ka?*
No more, thanks.	*Mō kek-kō de-su.*
It is(was) very delicious.	*To-te-mo o-i-shi-i de-su.*
Waiter!	*U-ē-tā san!*
Calling a waiter (or waitress)	You can say *"Su-mi-ma-sen,"* which means "I wish to have your attention for a moment."
Please bring it as possible as quickly.	*Ha-ya-ku mot-te ki-te ku-da-sa-i.*

The check, please.	*O-kan-jō o-ne-ga-i-shi-ma-su.*
Can I use my Diner's (Club) card?	*Da-i-nā-zu kā-do tsu-ka-e ma-su ka?*
I enjoyed it very much, thank you.	*Ta-i-hen ta-no-shi-kat-ta de-su.*
enjoyable	*ta-no-shi-i*
How do you like it?	*I-ka-ga de-su ka?*
How did you enjoy it?	*I-ka-ga de-shi-ta ka?*
I like it very much.	*Ta-i-hen su-ki de-su.*
I have made a reservation.	*Yo-ya-ku shi-ma-shi-ta.*
Shall we go?	*I-ki ma-shō ka?*
Let's go!	*I-ki ma-shō!*
I must go.	*O-i-to-ma shi-ma-su.*

VOCABULARY

Most Western drinks and dishes which you are used to are called by their original names, and if you pronounce them slowly without placing too much of an accent on any particular syllable, chances are that you will be understood in most cases.

appetite	*sho-ku-yo-ku*
banquet	*en-ka-i*
beef steak	*bi-i-fu su-tē-ki*
beer	*bi-i-ru*
black tea	*kō-cha*
bread	*pan*
breakfast	*a-sa go-han*
Chinese cuisine	*Chū-ka ryō-ri*
chopsticks	*ha-shi*
cold chicken	*kō-ru-do chi-kin*
cooked rice	*go-han*
dessert	*de-zā-to*
dining room	*sho-ku-dō*
dinner	*ban go-han*
dinner party	*yū-sho-ku ka-i*
dish, plate	*o-sa-ra*
drink *(n)*	*no-mi-mo-no*
drink *(v)*	*no-mu*
eat	*ta-be-ru*

fork	*fō-ku*
fried chicken	*fu-ra-i-do chi-kin*
fruit	*ku-da-mo-no; fu-rū-tsu*
grape juice	*gu-rē-pu jū-su*
green tea	*ryo-ku-cha*
ice	*kō-ri; a-i-su*
ice cream	*a-i-su ku-ri-i-mu*
Japanese cuisine	*Ni-hon ryō-ri*
Japanese tea	*Ni-hon cha*
knife	*na-i-fu*
lemon squash	*re-mon su-kas-shu*
lemonade	*re-mo-nē-do*
lunch	*hi-ru go-han*
lunch party	*chū-sho-ku ka-i*
meal	*sho-ku-ji*
milk	*mi-ru-ku*
mustard	*ka-ra-shi*
napkin	*na-pu-kin*
orange juice	*o-ren-ji jū-su*
party	*pā-ti-i*
pepper	*ko-shō*
pork chop	*pō-ku-chop-pu*

pork cutlet	*ton-ka-tsu*
raw fish	*sa-shi-mi*
roast chicken	*rō-su-to chi-kin*
roast beef	*rō-su-to bi-i-fu*
salad	*sa-ra-da*
salt	*shi-o*
sandwich	*san-do-wit-chi*
Scotch & soda	*Su-kot-chi sō-da*
Scotch & water	*Su-kot-chi u-ō-ta*
snack	*su-nak-ku*
soy sauce	*shō-yu*
spice	*ya-ku-mi*
spoon	*su-pūn*
sugar	*sa-tō*
table d'hote	*te-i-sho-ku*
(a la carte)	(*o-ko-no-mi ryō-ri*)
tea	*o-cha*
tea party	*ti-i pā-ti-i; o-cha-ka-i*
toast	*tō-su-to*
toothpick	*yō-ji*
waiter	*u-ē-tā*
waitress	*u-ē-to-re-su*
water	*o-mi-zu*

JAPANESE COOKING
(Ni-hon Ryo-ri)

We would like to explain a little bit about Japanese cooking. Three of the best known and most popular Japanese dishes are probably *SU-KI-YA-KI*, *TEM-PU-RA,* and *SU-SHI*.

SU-KI-YA-KI

Thin slices of beef are cooked together with different vegetables in an iron pan. The cooking is done in front of the guests. Japanese beef is said to be one of the most delicious types of beef in the world. *Kōbe* beef, *Matsuzaka* beef and *Ōmi* beef are three of the most famous sorts. In cooking *SU-KI-YA-KI*, opinions differ on whether the meat or vegetables are put in first, but let us leave that to the connoisseurs and enjoy the cooking. This dish is flavored with soy sauce and sugar.

TEM-PU-RA

Prawns, fish and vegetables are dipped in a thin batter (egg, water and flour) and deep-fried in vegetable oil. This is also cooked in front of the guests. The type of oil used by the cook is top secret. You will probably enjoy the prawns most of all. The prawns taste best when they are about the size of one's middle finger. They do not taste as good if they are bigger than this. The *TEM-PU-RA* is dipped in a soup which is made out of stock and soy sauce into which some grated radish may be added. Another way of eating it is to dip the *TEM-PU-RA* into a little salt mixed with *Ajinomoto* (monosodium glutamate) with a drop of lemon to spice it up.

Connoisseurs are supposed to dip the *TEM-PU-RA* only very slightly into the sauce, but we think it tastes much better with a lot of sauce. If you wish to look like a connoisseur, just dip the *TEM-PU-RA* in slightly and say, "Oh, that's good!" Then when you get the chance, soak it thoroughly and dig right in!

SU-SHI

This is a dish which may take a little time to acquire a taste for. However, with the Japanese people, it is one of the most popular of all foods. Perhaps only one in every million Japanese doesn't like it.

Slices of raw fish are placed on top of small balls of vinegared rice. This is dipped in soy sauce before being eaten. So great is the Japanese people's love of this dish that any Japanese who has been abroad for a few months will probably rush to a *SU-SHI* shop the moment he returns to Japan. Only after savouring some *SU-SHI* would he really feel that he was on home turf. Tuna is the best tasting *SU-SHI*. The rich fatty part of the tuna is called *To-ro*, while the lean section is called *Zu-ke*.

SHOPPING

If you have left your wife back at home, or if you cannot find time for an extensive shopping tour around town, just slip out and take a look at the shops located in the arcades of the major hotels. Many leading stores in Tokyo are represented in these locations, and a fine selection of almost anything a traveler would want to take home from Japan can be found there. The people working in these shops all speak some English.

If your schedule permits it, a visit to one of the larger department stores in Tokyo, or any other major city in Japan, may also be an interesting experience for you. The department stores, like in any other country, are stocked with every kind of merchandise under the sun. One of the unique features of a Japanese department store is the little park on the rooftop. Designed to attract the children (who, of course, bring their parents), these rooftops are equipped with all kinds of mechanical amusements and ice cream and candy stands. Some stores even have miniature zoos on the roof. Departments which you may want to visit include the kimono, camera, jewelry (pearls), toy (Japanese dolls and toys), art (popular wood-block prints and scrolls), ceramics and lacquer ware, music (CDs of Japanese instrumental music and folk songs), and umbrella (Japanese bamboo umbrellas and parasols) departments. If you need a haircut, a good barber shop can be found on the premises. All the big stores also have a photo studio where you can have your picture taken.

One should NOT try to bargain in department stores as all their prices are fixed. The only items that you can buy cheaper than the Japanese can are those articles which have been designated tax-free by the Government; namely, pearls, cameras, and binoculars.

Tokyo's leading department stores and their locations include:

Mitsukoshi	*(Nihonbashi, Ginza, Shinjuku and Ikebukuro)*
Takashimaya	*(Nihonbashi)*
Tokyu	*(Shibuya, Nihonbashi)*
Matsuya	*(Ginza and Asakusa)*

Matsuzakaya	*(Ginza* and *Ueno)*
Daimaru	(Tokyo Central Station Bldg.)
Isetan	*(Shinjuku)*
Odakyu	*(Shinjuku)*
Keio	*(Shinjuku)*
Seibu	*(Ikebukuro* and *Shibuya)*
Tobu	*(Ikebukuro)*

The bigger department stores may even have an English speaking guide who will take you around the store and help you shop. Just ask the receptionist on the ground floor whether this service is available. In case it is not, the following expressions will come in handy. All department stores are open on Sunday.

USEFUL PHRASES

shopping	*ka-i-mo-no*
I want to go shopping.	*Ka-i-mo-no shi-ta-i de-su.*

I am going shopping.	*Ka-i-mo-no ni i-ki-ma-su.*
window shopping	*u-in-dō shop-pin-gu su-ru*
Pardon me, but could you help me please?	*Chot-to o-ne-ga-i shi-ma-su.*
where	*do-ko*
Where is …?	*...... do-ko de-su ka?*
Where can I get ...?	*...... do-ko de ka-e-ma-su ka?*
department store	*de-pā-to*
Is it far from here?	*Ko-ko ka-ra tō-i de-su ka?*
How many minutes will it take from here?	*Ko-ko ka-ra nan-pun de-su ka?*
Please show me	*Mi-se-te ku-da-sa-i*
this	*ko-re*
that	*a-re*
Show me this, please.	*Ko-re mi-se-te ku-da-sa-i.*
Show me that, please.	*A-re mi-se-te ku-da-sa-i.*

What is this?	*Ko-re nan de-su ka?*
What is that?	*A-re nan de-su ka?*
How much?	*I-ku-ra de-su ka?*
How much is this?	*Ko-re i-ku-ra de-su ka?*
How much is that?	*A-re i-ku-ra de-su ka?*
It's expensive.	*Ta-ka-i de-su ne.*
It's cheap.	*Ya-su-i de-su ne.*
I want something cheaper.	*Mot-to ya-su-i no ku-da-sa-i.*
a big one	*ō-ki-i mo-no*
a small one	*chi-i-sa-i mo-no*
a larger one	*mot-to ō-ki-i mo-no*
a smaller one	*mot-to chi-i-sa-i mo-no*
a little	*su-ko-shi*
a lot	*ta-ku-san*
I'll take this one, please.	*Ko-re ku-da-sa-i.*
I'll take that one, thanks.	*A-re ku-da-sa-i.*
How old is this one?	*Ko-re do-no ku-ra-i fu-ru-i mo-no de-su ka?*

Do you have something better?	*Mot-to i-i-mo-no a-ri-ma-su ka?*
I like this.	*Ko-re ki-ni i-ri-ma-shi-ta.*
I don't like that.	*A-re ki-ni i-ri ma-sen.*
Will you come with me?	*Is-sho ni ki-te ku-da-sa-i.*
How much is it all together?	*Zen-bu de i-ku-ra de-su ka?*
Can I pay in ...?	*......de ha-rat-te i-i de-su ka?*
dollars	*do-ru*
travelers' cheques	*to-ra-be-rā chek-ku*
Diner's Club	*Da-i-nā-zu ku-ra-bu*
Can you send it to...?	*......ni o-kut-te ku-re-ma-su ka?*
U.S.A.	*A-me-ri-ka*
U.K.	*E-i-ko-ku*
France	*Fu-ran-su*
Germany	*Do-i-tsu*
Italy	*I-ta-ri-a*
Canada	*Ka-na-da*
Australia	*Ō-su-to-ra-ri-a*

air mail	*kō-kū-bin*
sea mail	*fu-na-bin*
Please give me the change.	*O-tsu-ri ku-da-sa-i.*
a receipt	*re-shi-i-to*
Please wrap it up.	*Tsu-tsun-de ku-da-sa-i.*
Please deliver it to my hotel.	*Ho-te-ru ni to-do-ke-te ku-da-sa-i.*
Please deliver it to my room.	*He-ya ni to-do-ke-te ku-da-sa-i.*
As soon as possible.	*De-ki-ru da-ke ha-ya-ku.*

VOCABULARY

arcade	*ā-ke-i-do*
art gallery	*ga-rō*
book	*hon*
book shop	*hon-ya*
butcher	*ni-ku-ya*

camera store	*ka-me-ra-ya*
chinaware store	*se-to-mo-no-ya*
curio shop	*kot-tō-ya*
dept. store	*de-pā-to*
dressmaker	*yō-sō-ten*
drug store	*ku-su-ri-ya*
fancy goods store	*yo-hin-ya*
florist	*ha-na-ya*
fruit store	*ku-da-mo-no-ya*
fur shop	*ke-ga-wa-ya*
furniture store	*ka-gu-ya*
greengrocer	*ya-o-ya*
grocery	*sho-ku-ryō-hin-ya*
hatter	*bō-shi-ya*
jeweller	*hō-se-ki-ya*
lacquer ware store	*shik-ki-ya*
laundry	*sen-ta-ku-ya*
pharmacy	*ku-su-ri-ya*
photo studio	*sha-shin-ya*
shoe store	*ku-tsu-ya*
souvenir shop	*mi-ya-ge-ya*
sporting goods store	*un-dō-gu-ya*
stationer	*bun-bō-gu-ya*

tailor	*yō-fu-ku-ya*
toy shop	*o-mo-cha-ya*
watch maker	*to-ke-i-ya*
woodblock print shop	*han-ga-ya*

SIGHTSEEING

There are so many places worth seeing in Japan. Most tourists who visit our country travel according to a detailed itinerary which takes care of all their needs. However, for those who don't, here is a short introduction to sightseeing "musts" in and beyond Tokyo.

TOKYO
1. *IMPERIAL PALACE*

Open to the public only twice a year (Jan. 2— New Year's, and Dec. 23—in celebration of the Emperor's Birthday). Features include moats, high stone walls and structures reminiscent of the feudal ages when the palace was known as *E-do* Castle. It was invincible stronghold of the *To-ku-ga-wa* who dominated Japan for 250 years. *E-do* Castle became the Imperial Palace in 1869, when Emperor *Me-i-ji* moved the capital from Kyoto to Tokyo. "Tokyo" means "Eastern Capital."

2. *ME-I-JI SHRINE*

Dedicated to the great Emperor *Me-i-ji*,

builder of the modern Japan, the impressive Shrine stands majestically in the center of 179 acres of heavily wooded grounds. Its famous Iris Garden is at its best in late June.

3. *ME-I-JI OUTER GARDEN*

Not far from the *Me-i-ji* Shrine lie 120 acres of parks and large public sports grounds, including the giant Olympic Stadium. A visit to the *Me-i-ji* Memorial Art Gallery *(KA-I-GA-KAN)* is also recommended. A collection of Japanese-style paintings and oils depicting historical events in the colorful life of Emperor *Me-i-ji* and the birth of modern Japan are also located here.

4. *A-SA-KU-SA KAN-NON (GODDESS OF MERCY) TEMPLE*

One of the rare spots in Tokyo where some of the jolly atmosphere of old Japan can still be found. Hundreds of colorful souvenir shops, shopping arcades, restaurants, stalls, and the theater alley—a street lined with theaters and cinemas—surround the temple.

5. *U-E-NO PARK*

a. National Museum

National treasures in paintings, calligraphy, textiles, ceramics, lacquer ware, metalwork and sculpture (changed periodically). Special exhibits are also held.

b. *U-e-no* Zoological Gardens

Open from 9:30 a.m. to 4:00 p.m. It is the largest and best equipped of all the zoos in Japan, covering an area of 31.2 acres. It will take about two hours to tour completely.

c. National Museum of Western Art

Erected in 1959, it houses the "*Ma-tsu-ka-ta* Collection," consisting of masterpieces of famous Western sculptors and painters, collected by the late *Kō-ji-rō Ma-tsu-ka-ta* (1865—1950), a business magnate, when he was in Europe in the early 1900's.

6. *GIN-ZA SHOPPING DISTRICT*

The *Gin-za* extends from *Kyō-ba-shi* to *Shin-ba-shi* and has some of the finest shops in the city. The streets behind the main *Ginza* strip are also lined with innumerable specialty shops.

7. *TOKYO TOWER*

It is near *Shi-ba* Park and belongs to the *Nip-pon* Television City Corporation. Built in 1958, it is 333m high and is said to be higher than the Eiffel Tower. You can get a bird's-eye view of Tokyo from the observation platforms which are 250m and 150m above ground level. The Tower houses a museum showing the latest developments in electronics, a shopping arcade, restaurants and amusement facilities.

8. *KA-BU-KI-ZA*

Reconstructed in 1950. This is where the classical *Ka-bu-ki* plays are enacted by the all-male *Ka-bu-ki* troupes. It is just off the *Gin-za* on the street to *Tsu-ki-ji*.

9. *SHIN-JU-KU GYO-EN (FORMERLY PRIVATE IMPERIAL GARDENS)*

Open to the public since the war.

beautiful during the cherry blossom and chrysanthemum seasons.

10. *KŌ-DŌ-KAN JŪ-DŌ HALL*

It may be interesting to drop in for half an hour to watch men and women, young and old, both foreign and Japanese, practicing *jūdō*, the world famous art of self-defense.

11. *A-KI-HA-BA-RA ELECTRICAL APPLI-ANCE AREA*

After World War II this area was notorious for its thriving black market but it has since been transformed into what is now a world-famous electrical appliance discount center. As soon as you step out of *A-ki-ha-ba-ra* station, you are bombarded with a myriad of garish neon signs and shop fronts, a mini tinsel-town in the heart of Tokyo. Stores are crammed with every electrical gadget imaginable. For music and electronics buffs, this is a must to see. Shop around before purchasing anything and try your hand at bartering; in *A-ki-ha-ba-ra* bargaining is commonplace.

12. *TOKYO DISNEYLAND*

Opened in 1983, this 46-hectare theme park is one of the largest of its kind in the world. Located in *U-ra-ya-su*, a mere 35 minute bus ride from Tokyo station, the Tokyo version of one of Walt Disney's dreamlands is a definite must for anyone in search of a great day out. Incorporating all of the most popular features of its American counterparts, Tokyo Disneyland blurs the distinction between being a kid and a adult. It has something for everyone and its five theme lands, Fantasyland, Westernland, Tomorrowland, Adventureland and World Bazaar, provide family entertainment at its best.

NIKKO

1. *TŌ-SHŌ-GŪ SHRINE*

A mausoleum built in honor of the first *To-ku-ga-wa Shō-gun, I-e-ya-su*, by his grandson, *I-e-mi-tsu*, in 1634. One of the most colorful and gorgeous shrines in all Japan. It should not be missed.

2. *LAKE CHŪ-ZEN-JI*

Eleven miles from *Nik-kō*, it lies 1269m above sea level. The drive up to the lake is beautiful and thrilling at any time of year.

3. *KE-GON FALLS*

One of the most beautiful waterfalls in the *Nik-kō* area, on the way to Lake *Chū-zen-ji*. The falls are 97m high, while the basin is 5m deep.

HAKONE

1. *Ō-WA-KU-DA-NI, KO-WA-KI-DA-NI (THE TWO HELLS)*

This area is famous for its sulphur hot springs. *Ko-wa-ki-da-ni* is a particularly popular sightseeing spot for cherry blossomes and azaleas when in bloom.

2. *LAKE A-SHI-NO-KO*

Lake *A-shi-no-ko* lies 725m above sea level and is 18km in circumference. A beautiful view of Mt. Fuji reflected in the water can be enjoyed on fine days.

3. *A-SHI-NO-KO SKYLINE DRIVE*

One of the most popular scenic drives in the Hakone area, this is a 11.7km toll road which leads from Hakone Pass to *Ko-ji-ri* on the northern shore of Lake *A-shi-no-ko* by way of the mountain ridges rising on the western shore of Lake *A-shi-no-ko* and *U-mi-ji-ri* Pass (alt:855m). This road affords fantastic views of the lake and Mt. Fuji, Sagami and Suruga Bays, and the Southern Japan Alps in the distance as it runs northwest over the summits of the Hakone range.

4. *HA-KO-NE SKYLINE AND HA-KO-NE TURNPIKE*

From *U-mi-ji-ri* Pass the road extends farther to *Na-ga-o* Pass and is called "Hakone Skyline." The other road is the "Hakone Turnpike," which runs for 13.8 km from *Yu-ga-wa-ra* Pass (Mt. Taikan) to *O-da-wa-ra*, following the mountain ridges south of the Hakone Bypass. Splendid views are afforded of the beautiful surrounding area.

GIFU

CORMORANT FISHING

(Catching fish with birds)

An unusual and picturesque sight is watching cormorants fish at night for *a-yu* (a kind of trout). Bonfires attached to the fishing boats light up the river and cormorant handlers dressed in traditional costumes work busily with their birds which they hold and control on the end of a long line. Fishing season is between May 11 and October 15.

TOBA

PEARL FARMING

The famous *Mi-ki-mo-to* pearl farms first started their production of cultured pearls here a century ago. Beautiful *A-go* Bay dotted with many islands is where the pearl farms are located.

KYOTO

The soft voice of feminine Kyoto will enchant you. The dialect is slightly differtent from the harsher Tokyo and Osaka dialects,

You will be welcomed into someone's home, a restaurant, or an inn with the gentle *O-I-DE YA-SU* (Please come in), thanked with a lilting *Ō-KI-NI*, and ushered out with a regretful *HA-YŌ O-KA-E-RI* (Please come back quickly.)

1. *HE-I-AN SHRINE*

Built in 1895 to commemorate the l,100th anniversary of the founding of Kyoto. Known for its beautiful garden at the back of the shrine. The weeping cherry trees in this garden are famous in Kyoto, and should not be missed when in bloom.

2. *SAN-JŪ-SAN-GEN-DŌ (TEMPLE OF THIRTY THREE SPACES)*

Original temple built in 1132 but rebuilt in 1251 after being destroyed by fire. Noted for the one thousand and one golden statues of the Goddess of Mercy. Main statue in center carved by *Tan-ke-i* at age of 82.

3. *KIN-KA-KU-JI (GOLDEN PAVILION)*

The present building is an exact reproduction of the former pavilion built in 1394, which was completely destroyed by fire in 1950. The new building was built in 1955.

4. *SA-I-HŌ-JI (MOSS TEMPLE)*

Garden known for beautiful moss. Over 100 varieties of moss can be found.

5. *RYŌ-AN-JI (ROCK GARDEN)*

Situated in the western suburbs of Kyoto. It was designed in 1473 by a Zen priest. Unique in the unusual use of rock, moss, and white sand.

6. *HO-ZU RAPIDS*

One and a half hour ride down the rapids in a flatbottom wooden boat maneuvered by three oarsmen offers a thrilling experience.

7. *NI-JŌ CASTLE*

Built in 1603 by the powerful lord *To-ku-ga-wa I-e-ya-su* and used as his headquarters in Kyoto. As a castle, it is one of the most ornately decorated structures in the country.

8. *SHIN-KYŌ-GO-KU*

Running parallel to *Ka-wa-ra-ma-chi* Street, it is one of the most picturesque shopping alleys in Kyoto. Especially picturesque at night when the shops are gaily lit. Shops are open till 10 o'clock.

9. *LACQUER FACTORY(ZŌ-HI-KO NI-SHI-MU-RA)*

The largest lacquer factory and show room in Japan near the *He-i-an* Shrine in the center of the city. The show room is a treasure house of antique lacquer ware.

10. *SILK GALLERIES*

Ta-tsu-mu-ra and *O-ri-do-no* are both stocked with beautiful silks and silk brocades. *Ta-tsu-mu-ra* is near the *Mi-ya-ko* Hotel and *O-ri-do-no* is almost next door to the Kyoto Hotel.

11. *ANTIQUES*

Fu-ru-mon-zen and *Shin-mon-zen* are lined with small antique and semi-antique shops.

Various other shops, selling kimonos, sword ornaments, wood-block prints, etc., can also be found on the same street.

NARA

1. *DA-I-BU-TSU*

The largest bronze Buddha to be found in Japan. Built in the eighth century, it has been repaired several times after having been destroyed by fire. The temple housing the Buddha is one of the largest wooden structures in the world.

2. *DEER PARK*

Tame deer roam the park and will eat out of your hand.

3. *KA-SU-GA SHRINE*

Erected in 768 by the *Fu-ji-wa-ra* family who was powerful when *Na-ra* was the capital of Japan before Kyoto. Stone lanterns donated by followers line the path leading to the shrine. Wisteria is particularly famous at the shrine.

4. *HŌ-RYŪ-JI*

The only group of wooden structures over

1200 years old remaining in the world. An almost complete compound of temple buildings stands intact here. It lies on the outskirts of *Nà-ra* on the road to Osaka.

Art treasures over 1200 years old can still be seen here.

USEFUL PHRASES

What are the places of interest here?	*Ko-ko no me-i-sho o-shi-e-te ku-da-sa-i.*
Where is the......?	*..... wa do-ko de-su ka?*
art gallery	*bi-ju-tsu-kan*
bar	*bā*
bridge	*ha-shi*
cabaret	*kya-ba-rē*
castle	*o-shi-ro*
church	*kyō-ka-i*
cinema	*e-i-ga-kan*
garden	*ni-wa*
harbor	*mi-na-to*

lake	*mi-zu-u-mi*
museum	*ha-ku-bu-tsu-kan*
nightclub	*na-i-to ku-ra-bu*
park	*kō-en*
pond	*i-ke*
river	*ka-wa*
sea	*u-mi*
shrine	*jin-ja*
temple	*o-te-ra*
theater	*ge-ki-jō*
university	*da-i-ga-ku*
Do you need a guide?	*Ga-i-do i-ri-ma-su ka?*
Yes, please.	*Ha-i, o-ne-ga-i shi-ma-su.*
Is there a guide here?	*Ga-i-do-san i-ma-su-ka?*
Is the museum open now (on Sunday)?	*Ha-ku-bu-tsu-kan (Ni-chi-yō-bi ni) a-i-te i-ma-su ka?*
How much is the admission?	*Nyū-jō-ryō i-ku-ra de-su ka?*
Is admission free?	*Nyū-jō-ryō ta-da de-su ka?*

Admission is ...... yen.	*Nyū-jō-ryō ... en de-su.*
It is closed on Monday.	*Ge-tsu-yō-bi shi-mat-te i-ma-su.*
May I take photographs?	*Sha-shin tot-te i-i de-su ka?*
Where is the entrance?	*I-ri-gu-chi do-ko de-su ka?*
Where are the theaters?	*Ge-ki-jō do-ko de-su ka?*
At what time does the performance start ?	*Nan-ji ni ha-ji-ma-ri ma-su ka?*
May I see your ticket please?	*Kip-pu mi-se-te ku-da-sa-i.*
What film is playing tonight?	*Kon-ban don-na e-i-ga yat-te i-ma-su ka?*
I would like to visit a nightclub.	*Na-i-to ku-ra-bu ni it-te mi-ta-i de-su.*
Where can we dance?	*O-do-re-ru to-ko-ro a-ri-ma-su ka?*
Is there a festival today ?	*Kyō o-ma-tsu-ri a-ri-ma-su ka ?*

125

Can I have a program please?	*Pu-ro-gu-ra-mu ku-da-sa-i.*
I would like to catch a taxi.	*Ta-ku-shi-i o-ne-ga-i-shi-ma-su.*
I would like to hire a car.	*Ha-i-yā o-ne-ga-i-shi-ma-su.*
How much is it to ....?	*.... ma-de i-ku-ra de-su ka?*
How much is it for the whole day?	*I-chi-ni-chi ka-shi-ki-ri de i-ku-ra de-su ka?*
How much is it for half a day?	*Han-ni-chi ka-shi-ki-ri de i-ku-ra de-su ka?*
left	*hi-da-ri*
right	*mi-gi*
Turn to the left.	*Hi-da-ri ni ma-gat-te ku-da-sa-i.*
Turn to the right.	*Mi-gi ni ma-gat-te ku-da-sa-i.*
Go straight ahead.	*Mas-su-gu it-te ku-da-sa-i.*
Stop.	*To-mat-te ku-da-sa-i.*

WEATHER

127

The climate in Japan is more or less like that of New York with its hot summers, cold winters, warm springs, and cool autumns.

In spring we have the world-famous cherry blossoms, while in autumn the mountains are ablaze with the beautiful autumn-colored maples. We suggest that if you intend to come to Japan for sightseeing or for pleasure, come either in spring or autumn.

USEFUL PHRASES

How is the weather?	*O-ten-ki dō de-su ka?*
It is good (bad, hot, cold, cool).	*I-i (wa-ru-i, a-tsu-i, sa-mu-i, su-zu-shi-i) de-su.*
It is a fine day today.	*Kyō wa i-i o-ten-ki de-su.*
It has started to snow (rain).	*Yu-ki (a-me) ga fu-ri ha-ji-me ma-shi-ta.*
It is raining (snowing, hailing).	*A-me (yu-ki, hyō) ga fut-te i-ma-su.*
The sun is shining.	*Hi ga de-te i-ma-su.*
It's nice weatner.	*I-i o-ten-ki de-su.*

The stars are out.	*Ho-shi ga de-te i-ma-su.*
Do you feel cold?	*Sa-mu-i de-su ka?*
I feel warm.	*A-ta-ta-ka-i de-su.*
I am sleepy.	*Ne-mu-i de-su.*
It is too cold (hot) to go out today.	*Kyō wa de-ka-ke-ru no ni sa-mu (a-tsu) su-gi ma-su.*
I don't like the cold (heat, rain, snow, wind, cloudy weather).	*Sa-mu-i no (a-tsu-i no, a-me, yu-ki, ka-ze, ku-mo-ri) wa ki-ra-i de-su.*
It looks like it's going to rain.	*A-me ga fu-ri sō de-su ne.*
It's going to clear up.	*Ha-re sō de-su.*
It will be fine tomorrow.	*A-shi-ta wa ha-re de shō.*
I am terribly wet.	*Bi-sho-nu-re de-su.*
When do the cherry blossoms bloom?	*Sa-ku-ra wa i-tsu sa-ki-ma-su ka?*
The spring is beautiful in Kyoto.	*Kyō-to no ha-ru wa ki-re-i de-su.*
What is today's weather forecast?	*Kyō no ten-ki yo-hō wa dō de-su-ka?*

VOCABULARY

clear (day)	*ha-re*
climate	*ki-kō*
cloud	*ku-mo*
cloudy	*ku-mo-ri*
cold	*sa-mu-i*
cool	*su-zu-shi-i*
damp	*shi-mep-po-i*
drought	*hi-de-ri*
earthquake*	*ji-shin*
fine (day)	*ha-re*
flood	*kō-zu-i*
fog	*ki-ri*
frost	*shi-mo*
hail	*hyō or a-ra-re*
haze	*mo-ya*
hot	*a-tsu-i*
lightning	*i-na-bi-ka-ri*
rain	*a-me*
rainbow	*ni-ji*
shower	*ni-wa-ka a-me*
sleet	*mi-zo-re*

snow	*yu-ki*
storm	*a-ra-shi*
sultry	*mu-shi-a-tsu-i*
sunstroke	*nis-sha byō*
thunder	*ka-mi-na-ri*
typhoon	*ta-i-fū*
weather	*o-ten-ki*
wind	*ka-ze*
windy	*ka-ze ga tsu-yo-i*

*Earthquakes are feared very much in Japan. There is an old proverb in Japanese which goes:

"*JI-SHIN, KA-MI-NA-RI, KA-JI, O-YA-JI*"
(Earthquake) (Thunder) (Fire) (the old
                                    man—father)

These represent the four most feared phenomena in Japan in order of their fearfulness.

TIME, DAYS OF THE WEEK, MONTHS AND SEASONS

TIME

1 o'clock	*I-chi ji*
2 o'clock	*Ni ji*
3 o'clock	*San ji*
4 o'clock	*Yo ji*
5 o'clock	*Go ji*
6 o'clock	*Ro-ku ji*
7 o'clock	*Shi-chi ji*
8 o'clock	*Ha-chi ji*
9 o'clock	*Ku ji*
10 o'clock	*Jū ji*
11 o'clock	*Jū-i-chi ji*
12 o'clock	*Jū-ni ji*

1 a.m.	*Go-zen i-chi ji*
1 p.m.	*Go-go i-chi ji*
Half past one	*I-chi ji han* (one o'clock half)
Quarter past one	*I-chi ji jū-go fun su-gi* (one o'clock fifteen minutes past)
Quarter to one	*I-chi ji jū-go fun ma-e*

(One o'clock fifteen
minutes before)

What time is it now?	*I-ma nan-ji de-su ka?*
It is one o'clock	*I-chi ji de-su.*
I saw him yesterday.	*Ki-nō a-i-ma-shi-ta.*
yesterday	*ki-nō*
last night	*yū-be*
the day before yesterday	*o-to-to-i*
last year	*kyo-nen*
last month	*sen ge-tsu*
last week	*sen-shū*
three days ago	*mik-ka ma-e*
three years ago	*san nen ma-e*
in 1990	*sen kyū-hya-ku* *kyū-jū-nen ni*
I shall see him today.	*Kyō a-i-ma-su.*
today	*kyō*
tonight	*kon-ban*
this morning	*ke-sa*
this afternoon	*kyō no go-go*
this evening	*kon-ban*
tomorrow	*a-shi-ta*

135

tomorrow morning	*a-su no a-sa*
tomorrow afternoon	*a-su no go-go*
tomorrow evening (night)	*a-su no ban*
the day after tomorrow	*a-sat-te*
next year	*ra-i-nen*
next month	*ra-i-ge-tsu*
next week	*ra-i-shū*
in a few days	*ni-san ni-chi chū ni*
I see him every day (week, month).	*Ma-i-ni-chi (ma-i-shū, ma-i-tsu-ki) a-i ma-su.*

DAYS OF THE WEEK

The days of the week are named after the sun, moon, and planets.

Sunday	*Ni-chi-yō*	(Sun-day)
Monday	*Ge-tsu-yō*	(Moon-day)
Tuesday	*Ka-yō*	(Mars-day)

Wednesday	*Su-i-yō*	(Mercury-day)
Thursday	*Mo-ku-yō*	(Jupiter-day)
Friday	*Kin-yō*	(Venus-day)
Saturday	*Do-yō*	(Saturn-day)

What day is it today? *Kyō wa nan-yō de-su ka?*

Today is ...... *Kyō wa .... de-su.*

MONTHS & SEASONS OF THE YEAR

In Japan it is very easy to count the months, as we just say first month, second month, third month, and so forth.

January	*I-chi-ga-tsu*
February	*Ni-ga-tsu*
March	*San-ga-tsu*
April	*Shi-ga-tsu*
May	*Go-ga-tsu*
June	*Ro-ku-ga-tsu*
July	*Shi-chi-ga-tsu*
August	*Ha-chi-ga-tsu*
September	*Ku-ga-tsu*

October	*Jū-ga-tsu*
November	*Jū-i-chi-ga-tsu*
December	*Jū-ni-ga-tsu*

When were you here last?	*Ma-e wa i-tsu ki-ta no de-su ka?*
I was here in the month of	*...... ni ki-ma-shi-ta.*
What is today's date?	*Kyō wa nan-ni-chi de-su ka?*
Today is the first of July.	*Kyō wa Shi-chi-ga-tsu tsu-i-ta-chi de-su.*

1st	*tsu-i-ta-chi*
2nd	*fu-tsu-ka*
3rd	*mik-ka*
4th	*yok-ka*
5th	*i-tsu-ka*
6th	*mu-i-ka*
7th	*na-no-ka*
8th	*yō-ka*
9th	*ko-ko-no-ka*
10th	*tō-ka*
11th	*jū-i-chi-ni-chi*

20th	*ha-tsu-ka*
21st	*ni-jū-i-chi-ni-chi*
30th	*san-jū-ni-chi*
31st	*san-jū-i-chi-ni-chi*
The spring is beautiful in Japan.	*Nip-pon no ha-ru wa u-tsu-ku-shi-i de-su.*
spring	*ha-ru*
summer	*na-tsu*
autumn	*a-ki*
winter	*fu-yu*

NUMERALS
AND
WAYS OF
COUNTING

In Japan one of the most complicated and difficult things to learn is the correct way of counting various items. For instance:

	One	Two	Three
people	*hi-to-ri*	*fu-ta-ri*	*san-nin*
cats, dogs	*ip-pi-ki*	*ni-hi-ki*	*san-bi-ki*
cattle, horses	*it-tō*	*ni-tō*	*san-tō*
sticks, pencils trees, bottles, lines }	*ip-pon*	*ni-hon*	*san-bon*
sheets of paper	*i-chi-ma-i*	*ni-ma-i*	*san-ma-i*
cars, trains, bicycles }	*i-chi-da-i*	*ni-da-i*	*san-da-i*
birds, rabbits	*i-chi-wa*	*ni-wa*	*san-ba*
chopsticks	*i-chi-zen*	*ni-zen*	*san-zen*
flowers	*i-chi-rin*	*ni-rin*	*san-rin*
houses	*ik-ken*	*ni-ken*	*san-gen*
cupful and bowlful }	*ip-pa-i*	*ni-ha-i*	*san-ba-i*
books, note-books }	*is-sa-tsu*	*ni-sa-tsu*	*san-sa-tsu*
apples, peaches	*ik-ko*	*ni-ko*	*san-ko*

sets	*hi-to-ku-mi*	*fu-ta-ku-mi*	*mi-ku-mi*
boats	*ip-pa-i*	*ni-ha-i*	*san-ba-i*
	is-sō	*ni-sō*	*san-sō*
	is-se-ki	*ni-se-ki*	*san-se-ki*

However, we are giving you the most usual and common way of counting so that you will not be too disheartened. You can always say, when counting different items, *"hi-to-tsu, fu-ta-tsu, mit-tsu,"* and when counting numbers, *"i-chi, ni, san."*

NUMERALS

	Cardinals	Counting Units	Japanese Characters
One	*i-chi**	*hi-to-tsu* (one unit)*	一
Two	*ni*	*fu-ta-tsu*	二
Three	*san*	*mit-tsu*	三
Four	*shi*	*yot-tsu*	四
Five	*go*	*i-tsu-tsu*	五
Six	*ro-ku*	*mut-tsu*	六

Seven	*shi-chi*	*na-na-tsu*	七
Eight	*ha-chi*	*yat-tsu*	八
Nine	*kyū* or *ku*	*ko-ko-no-tsu*	九
Ten	*jū*	*tō*	十

*Examples:

One pack of ciga- rettes	*ta-ba-ko hi-to-tsu* (not *i-chi ta-ba-ko*)
Two hot dogs	*hot-to dog-gu fu-ta-tsu*
Three ice creams	*a-i-su ku-ri-i-mu mit-tsu*

From eleven onwards, counting units become the same as the cardinals.

Eleven	*jū-i-chi*
Twelve	*jū-ni*
Thirteen	*jū-san*
Fourteen	*jū-shi*
Fifteen	*jū-go*
Sixteen	*jū-ro-ku*
Seventeen	*jū-shi-chi*
Eighteen	*jū-ha-chi*
Nineteen	*jū-ku*

Twenty	*ni-jū*
Twenty-one (two ten one)	*ni-jū-i-chi*
Twenty-two (two ten two)	*ni-jū-ni*
Thirty (three ten)	*san-jū*
Thirty-one (three ten one)	*san-jū-i-chi*
Thirty-two (three ten two)	*san-jū-ni*
Forty (four ten)	*yon-jū*
Fifty (five ten)	*go-jū*
Sixty (six ten)	*ro-ku-jū*
Seventy (seven ten)	*shi-chi-jū*
Eighty (eight ten)	*ha-chi-jū*
Ninety (nine ten)	*kyū-jū*
One hundred	*hya-ku*
One hundred and one	*hya-ku-i-chi*
One hundred and ten	*hya-ku-jū*
One hundred and twenty	*hya-ku-ni-jū*
One hundred and thirty-one	*hya-ku-san-jū-i-chi*

Two hundred	*ni-hya-ku*
Four hundred	*yon-hya-ku*
Six hundred	*rop-pya-ku*
Eight hundred	*hap-pya-ku*
One thousand	*sen*
Three thousand	*san-zen*
Seven thousand	*na-na-sen*
Eight thousand	*has-sen*
Ten thousand	*i-chi-man*
Eleven thousand	*i-chi-man-is-sen*
Hundred thousand	*jū-man*
One million	*hya-ku-man*
One billion	*jū-o-ku*

ORDINALS

First	*i-chi ban*
Second	*ni ban*
Third	*san ban*
Fourth	*yon ban*
Fifth	*go ban*
Sixth	*ro-ku ban*

Seventh	*na-na ban; shi-chi ban*
Eighth	*ha-chi ban*
Ninth	*kyū ban*
Tenth	*jū ban*
Eleventh	*jū-i-chi ban*
Half	*han-bun*
One quarter	*yon-bun-no-i-chi*
Once	*i-chi do*
Twice	*ni do*
Three times	*san do*
The first time	*ha-ji-me-te*
The second time	*ni ka-i me*
The third time	*san ka-i me*
The last time	*sa-i-go; sa-i-kin*
One dozen	*i-chi dā-su*

JUST FOR
YOUR
INFORMATION

BO-KU
Little Boys

GU-SŌ
Buddhist Priests

SES-SHA
Samrai Warriors

WA-RA-WA
Princesses

WA-SHI
Elder Men

A-TA-SHI
Little Girls

O-RE
Certain Youths

WA-TA-KU-SHI
Young Ladies

U-CHI
Young Girls from Kyoto

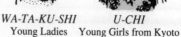

A HUNDRED WAYS OF SAYING "I" !

There are close to a hundred ways of saying "I" or "me" in Japanese. That's why Japanese can be one of the most difficult languages in the world to master. There are different "I"s for men and women, young and old, city folk and country folk, members of upper class families and those of lower class families; different "I"s used according to situations (such as among friends, addressing subordinates or superiors); special "I"s that one uses in correspondence; and "I"s used in different ages of the past, etc. But the only "I" you should or need to learn is:

"WA-TA-KU-SHI "

Just for fun, let us give you some of the different Japanese "I"s that we can think of. We are sure that if we asked a language professor, he or she would come up with some more.

LIST OF "I" S IN JAPANESE

1. A
2. A-i
3. A-ko
4. A-re
5. A-shi
6. As-shi
7. A-ta-i
8. A-ta-ki
9. A-ta-ku-shi
10. A-ta-shi
11. A-te
12. Bo-ku
13. Chin
14. Da-i-kō
15. Da-ra
16. Fu-bin
17. Fu-ko-ku
18. Fu-shō
19. Ge-kan
20. Ge-se-tsu
21. Ge-shō
22. Gi-ra
23. Go-jin
24. Gu
25. Gu-se-i
26. Gu-sō
27. Hi-shō
28. Hon-kan
29. Hon-sho-ku
30. I-gi
31. In
32. Ji-bun
33. Ka-jin
34. Ken-ge
35. Ko-chi
36. Ko-chi-to
37. Ko-chi-to-ra
38. Kō-do
39. Ko-ko-mo-to
40. Ko-na-ta
41. Ma-ro
42. Mi
43. Mi-do-mo
44. Mi-zu-ka-ra
45. Na-ni-ga-shi
46. O
47. O-i-don
48. O-i-ra
49. O-no
50. O-no-re
51. O-ra
52. O-re
53. O-re-ra
54. O-ta-ki
55. Ra
56. Ses-sha
57. Se-tsu

58. *Shō*
59. *Shō-kan*
60. *Shō-se-i*
61. *Shō-shi*
62. *Shō-te-i*
63. *Sō*
64. *So-re ga-*
    shi
65. *Te-ma-e*
66. *Tō-hō*
67. *Tō-sho-ku*
68. *U-chi*
69. *Ura*
70. *U-se-i*

71. *U-se-tsu*
72. *Wa*
73. *Wa-chi-ki*
74. *Wa-ga-*
    ha-i
75. *Wa-ga-mi*
76. *Wa-i*
77. *Wa-ki*
78. *Wa-na-mi*
79. *Wan-de-*
    ra
80. *Wa-ra-wa*
81. *Wa-re*
82. *Wa-shi*

83. *Wa-ta-i*
84. *Wa-ta-ku-*
    shi
85. *Wa-ta-shi*
86. *Wa-te*
87. *Ya-ra*
88. *Ya-se-i*
89. *Ya-se-tsu*
90. *Ya-tsu-*
    ga-re
91. *Yo*
92. *Yo-ha-i*
93. *Yo-no-*
    mon

"I" AND "YOU"

When you are speaking to any Japanese, male or female, young or old, married or single, always address them with a *"san"* after their name. Never use *"san"* when you talk about yourself or any member of your family, as *"san"* is a suffix of respect.

Modesty and humility have always been regarded as very important virtues of people in this part of the world, and many Japanese manners and customs reflect this philosophy. Extreme self-deprecation, however, is gradually going out the window. The Japanese people are waking up to the idea of equal rights of the individual and the equality of the sexes.

However, modesty is still considered a virtue in the eyes of the Japanese people. For instance, you might receive a gift from a Japanese friend who will invariably call it "a very poor and cheap gift" or "only a very small souvenir." If you find a pearl brooch in the package, don't think they are fake pearls even if your friend has said it is a "cheap" article. It is quite possible that they are expensive *MIKIMOTO* pearls. When you are invited for dinner, the host may say to you "There is really nothing to eat, but please help yourself." Don't worry, there will be plenty on the table.

EXAMPLES

Please give my re-gards to your wife.	*O-ku-sa-ma ni yo-ro-shi-ku.*
Best regards from my wife.	*Ka-na-i ka-ra yo-ro-shi-ku.*

wife
   (1) the other's wife   *o-ku-sa-ma*

   (2) your own wife   *ka-na-i*

husband
- (1) the other's husband   *go-shu-jin sa-ma*
- (2) your own husband   *shu-jin*

Mr., Mrs. & Miss......   ...... *san*

e.g.   Mr. Enoch   Enoch-*san*
      Mrs. Stedman   Stedman-*san*
      Miss Meyer   Meyer-*san*

JAPANESE NAMES

Many surnames, like some in English, describe a location where, perhaps, the first ancestors lived when the name was created.

FUKUDA	Lucky rice field
HONDA	Main rice field
IKEDA	Pond and rice field
ISHIBASHI	Stone bridge
KINOSHITA	Under the tree

KOJIMA	Little island
KOYAMA	Little mountain
KURIHARA	Chestnut tree plain
MATSUSHITA	Under the pine tree
MITSUI	Three wells
NAGASHIMA	Eternal island
NAKAMURA	Inner village
NOMURA	Village in the field
OGAWA	Little stream
TANAKA	Inside the rice field
TOYODA	Abundant rice field
WATANABE	Settler
YAMADA	Mountain rice field
YAMASHITA	Under the mountain

Most given names of Japanese women end in one of the three following suffixes: "......ko," "....e" and "....yo."

e.g. *Masako* *Michiko* *Naoko*
     Masae *Michie* *Naoe*
     Masayo *Michiyo* *Naoyo*

VOCABULARY

MAMMALS ....*ho-nyū-ru-i*

animal ....*dō-bu-tsu*
domestic animal....*ka-chi-ku*
zoo ....*dō-bu-tsu-en*

anteater	*a-ri-ku-i*
antelope	*ka-mo-shi-ka*
baboon	*hi-hi*
bat	*kō-mo-ri*
bear	*ku-ma*
beaver	*bi-i-bā*
bison	*ya-gyū*
buffalo	*su-i-gyū*
camel	*ra-ku-da*
cat	*ne-ko*
cheetah	*chi-i-tā*
chimpanzee	*chin-pan-ji-i*
cow	*me-u-shi*
deer	*shi-ka*
dog	*i-nu*
dolphin	*i-ru-ka*
elephant	*zō*
fox	*ki-tsu-ne*
giraffe	*ki-rin*
goat	*ya-gi*
gorilla	*go-ri-ra*
hedgehog	*ha-ri-ne-zu-mi*
hippopotamus	*ka-ba*

horse	*u-ma*
hyena	*ha-i-e-na*
kangaroo	*kan-ga-rū*
koala	*ko-a-ra*
leopard	*hyō*
lion	*ra-i-on*
llama	*ra-ma*
mole	*mo-gu-ra*
monkey	*sa-ru*
mouse	*ha-tsu-ka-ne-zu-mi*
orangutan	*o-ran-ū-tan*
otter	*ka-wa-u-so*
ox	*o-u-shi*
pig	*bu-ta*
porcupine	*ya-ma-a-ra-shi*
rabbit	*u-sa-gi*
raccoon	*a-ra-i-gu-ma*
rat	*ne-zu-mi*
rhinoceros	*sa-i*
seal	*a-za-ra-shi*
sheep	*hi-tsu-ji*
sloth	*na-ma-ke-mo-no*
squirrel	*ri-su*
stag	*o-ji-ka*
tiger	*to-ra*
weasel	*i-ta-chi*
wolf	*ō-ka-mi*
zebra	*shi-ma-u-ma*

BIRDS ....*to-ri*

bill, beak.................*ku-chi-ba-shi*
bird-cage ....*to-ri ka-go*
feathers..................*ha-ne*
feed........................*e-sa*
fly...........................*to-bu*

bird of paradise	*go-ku-ra-ku-chō*
buzzard	*ha-ge-ta-ka*
canary	*ka-na-ri-a*
chick	*hi-na*
chicken	*ni-wa-to-ri*
crane	*tsu-ru*
crow	*ka-ra-su*
cuckoo	*kak-kō*
dove	*ya-ma-ba-to*
duck	*a-hi-ru*
eagle	*wa-shi*
falcon	*ha-ya-bu-sa*
goose	*ga-chō*
hawk	*ta-ka*
hen	*men-do-ri*
heron	*sa-gi*
kingfisher	*ka-wa-se-mi*
lark	*hi-ba-ri*
love-bird	*jū-shi-ma-tsu*
magpie	*ka-sa-sa-gi*

nightingale	*u-gu-i-su*
owl	*fu-ku-rō*
parakeet	*in-ko*
parrot	*ō-mu*
peacock	*ku-ja-ku*
pelican	*pe-ri-kan*
penguin	*pen-gin*
pheasant	*ki-ji*
pigeon	*ha-to*
quail	*u-zu-ra*
robin	*ko-ma-do-ri*
rooster	*on-do-ri*
sea gull	*ka-mo-me*
sparrow	*su-zu-me*
starling	*mu-ku-do-ri*
swallow	*tsu-ba-me*
swan	*ha-ku-chō*
thrush	*tsu-gu-mi*
turkey	*shi-chi-men-chō*
wagtail	*se-ki-re-i*
wild duck	*ka-mo*
wood pecker	*ki-tsu-tsu-ki*

FISH......................*sa-ka-na*

aquarium ....*su-i-zo-ku-kan*
fin ....*hi-re*
fishing ....*tsu-ri*
gill ....*e-ra*
lake ....*mi-zu-u-mi*
pond ....*i-ke*
river ....*ka-wa*
sea ....*u-mi*
swim ....*o-yo-gu*

Sea Fish ....*u-mi no sa-ka-na*

bonito	*ka-tsu-o*
cod	*ta-ra*
crab	*ka-ni*
cuttlefish	*i-ka*
flatfish	*hi-ra-me*
flying fish	*to-bi-u-o*
globefish	*fu-gu*
hermit crab	*ya-do-ka-ri*
herring	*ni-shin*
horse mackerel	*a-ji*
jellyfish	*ku-ra-ge*
lobster	*i-se-e-bi*
mackerel	*sa-ba*

mackerelpike	*san-ma*
octopus	*ta-ko*
oyster	*ka-ki*
prawn	*ku-ru-ma-e-bi*
sea bream	*ta-i*
sea eel	*a-na-go*
tuna	*ma-gu-ro*
whitebait	*shi-ra-u-o*
wreath shell	*sa-za-e*
yellowtail	*bu-ri*

River Fish............*ka-wa no sa-ka-na*

ayu (sweet-fish)	*a-yu*
carp	*ko-i*
catfish	*na-ma-zu*
crawfish	*za-ri-ga-ni*
eel	*u-na-gi*
goby	*ha-ze*
goldfish	*kin-gyo*
killifish	*me-da-ka*
loach	*do-jō*
pike	*ka-wa-ka-ma-su*
pond snail	*ta-ni-shi*
rainbow trout	*ni-ji-ma-su*
red trout	*be-ni-ma-su*
roach	*fu-na*

163

salmon	*sa-ke*
trout	*ma-su*
young salmon	*ya-ma-me*

AMPHIBIANS..... *su-i-ri-ku ryō-se-i-ru-i*

creepy feeling.......*ki-mi ga wa-ru-i*
croak ....*gā-gā na-ku*
jump ....*to-bu*
swim ....*o-yo-gu*

frog	*ka-e-ru*
salamander	*san-shō-u-o*
tadpole	*o-ta-ma-ja-ku-shi*
toad	*ga-ma*

REPTILES............*ha-chū-ru-i*

crawl ....*ha-u*
dangerous ....*ki-ken na*
fearful ....*ko-wa-i*

alligator	*wa-ni*
crocodile	*wa-ni*
gecko	*ya-mo-ri*
lizard	*to-ka-ge*

snake	*he-bi*
snapping turtle	*sup-pon*
tortoise	*ka-me*
turtle	*ka-me*

INSECTS ....*kon-chū; mu-shi*

bite	*sa-su*
catch	*to-ru*
collect....................	*shū-shū; a-tsu-me-ru*
crawl......................	*ha-u*
fly..........................	*to-bu*
net..........................	*a-mi*
sing........................	*na-ku*
smell......................	*ku-sa-i*

ant	*a-ri*
bedbug	*nan-kin mu-shi*
bee	*ha-chi*
beetle	*ka-bu-to mu-shi*
bookworm	*shi-mi*
butterfly	*chō-chō*
cicada	*se-mi*
centipede	*mu-ka-de*
cricket	*kō-ro-gi*
dragonfly	*ton-bo*
firefly	*ho-ta-ru*
flea	*no-mi*

fly	*ha-e*
gnat	*bu-yo*
grasshopper	*bat-ta*
hornet	*ku-ma-ba-chi*
ladybug	*ten-tō mu-shi*
locust	*i-na-go*
lice	*shi-ra-mi*
praying mantis	*ka-ma-ki-ri*
mosquito	*ka*
moth	*ga*
pondskater	*a-men-bō*
scorpion	*sa-so-ri*
spider	*ku-mo*
swallowtail	*a-ge-ha-chō*
tick	*da-ni*
water spider	*mi-zu-su-ma-shi*
weevil	*zō-mu-shi*

FLOWERS..........*ha-na*
        &
TREES ....*ki*

branch	*e-da*
garden	*ni-wa*
leaf	*hap-pa*
plant......................	*u-e-ru*
root.......................	*ne*

166

azalea	*tsu-tsu-ji*
baby's breath	*ka-su-mi-sō*
bamboo	*ta-ke*
camellia	*tsu-ba-ki*
carnation	*kā-nē-shon*
cherry blossoms	*sa-ku-ra*
Chinese bellflower	*ki-kyō*
chrysanthemum	*ki-ku*
cosmos	*ko-su-mo-su*
cryptomeria	*su-gi*
cyclamen	*shi-ku-ra-men*
cypress	*hi-no-ki*
daffodil	*sui-sen*
dahlia	*da-ri-a*
daisy	*no-gi-ku*
dandelion	*tan-po-po*
evening primrose	*tsu-ki-mi-sō*
gingko tree	*i-chō*
gladiolus	*gu-ra-ji-o-ra-su*
iris	*a-ya-me; shō-bu*
lily	*yu-ri*
lily of the valley	*su-zu-ran*
magnolia	*mo-ku-ren*
maple	*mo-mi-ji*
morning glory	*a-sa-ga-o*
oak	*ka-shi*
orchid	*ran*
peach blossoms	*mo-mo*

pine	*ma-tsu*
pink	*na-de-shi-ko*
plum blossoms	*u-me*
poppy	*ke-shi*
primrose	*sa-ku-ra-sō*
rose	*ba-ra*
sunflower	*hi-ma-wa-ri*
sweet flag	*a-ya-me*
sweet pea	*su-i-i-to-pi-i*
tulip	*chū-rip-pu*
violet	*su-mi-re*
walnut tree	*ku-ru-mi*
water lily	*su-i-ren*
wisteria	*fu-ji*
willow	*ya-na-gi*
zinnia	*hya-ku-ni-chi-sō*

VEGETABLES ..*ya-sa-i*
&
FRUITS ....*ku-da-mo-no*

apple	*rin-go*
apricot	*an-zu*
asparagus	*a-su-pa-ra-ga-su*
bamboo sprout	*ta-ke-no-ko*
banana	*ba-na-na*
beans	*in-gen*
bean sprout	*mo-ya-shi*

168

beet	*bi-i-to*
brussels sprout	*me-kya-be-tsu*
cabbage	*kya-be-tsu*
carrot	*nin-jin*
cauliflower	*ka-ri-fu-ra-wā*
celery	*se-ro-ri*
cherry	*sa-ku-ran-bo*
chestnut	*ku-ri*
corn	*tō-mo-ro-ko-shi*
cucumber	*kyū-ri*
eggplant	*na-su*
fig	*i-chi-ji-ku*
garlic	*nin-ni-ku*
ginger	*shō-ga*
grape	*bu-dō*
grapefruit	*gu-rē-pu fu-rū-tsu*
icicle radish	*da-i-kon*
lemon	*re-mon*
lettuce	*re-ta-su*
loquat	*bi-wa*
lotus	*ha-su*
mushrooms	*ki-no-ko*
mustard	*ka-ra-shi*
olive	*o-ri-i-bu*
onion	*ta-ma-ne-gi*
orange	*o-ren-ji*
peach	*mo-mo*
pear	*na-shi*

peppers	*pi-i-man*
persimmon	*ka-ki*
pineapple	*pa-i-nap-pu-ru*
plum	*u-me*
pomegranate	*za-ku-ro*
potato	*ja-ga-i-mo*
prune	*pu-rūn*
raisins	*ho-shi-bu-dō*
soybean	*da-i-zu*
spinach	*hō-ren-sō*
strawberry	*i-chi-go*
string bean	*sa-ya-ma-me*
sweet potato	*sa-tsu-ma-i-mo*
tangerine	*mi-kan*
taro	*sa-to-i-mo*
tomato	*to-ma-to*
turnip	*ka-bu*
walnut	*ku-ru-mi*
watermelon	*su-i-ka*

SOME GEOGRAPHICAL TERMS

Atlantic	*Ta-i-se-i-yō*
bay	*wan*
city	*to-ka-i*
forest	*mo-ri*
hot spring	*on-sen*

170

island	*shi-ma*
lake	*mi-zu-u-mi*
land	*ri-ku*
North Pole	*Hok-kyo-ku*
ocean	*u-mi*
Pacific	*Ta-i-he-i-yō*
peninsula	*han-tō*
pond	*i-ke*
river	*ka-wa*
sea	*u-mi*
sky	*so-ra*
South Pole	*Nan-kyo-ku*
town	*ma-chi*
village	*mu-ra*
waterfall	*ta-ki*

MINERALS ....*kō-bu-tsu*

coal	*se-ki-tan*
copper	*dō*
gold	*kin*
iron	*te-tsu*
lead	*na-ma-ri*
silver	*gin*
steel	*ha-ga-ne*
tin	*su-zu*

SPACE ....*u-chū*

earth	*chi-kyū*
comet	*hō-ki-bo-shi*
Jupiter	*mo-ku-se-i*
Mars	*ka-se-i*
Mercury	*su-i-se-i*
moon	*tsu-ki*
Plow	*ho-ku-to shi-chi-se-i*
pole star	*hok-kyo-ku-sei*
Saturn	*do-se-i*
star	*ho-shi*
sun	*ta-i-yō*
Venus	*kin-se-i*

COLORS ....*i-ro*

bright	....................*ha-de*
dark	......................*ko-i*
light	......................*u-su-i*
subdued	...............*ji-mi*

black	*ku-ro*
blue	*a-o*
brown	*cha-i-ro*
golden	*kin-i-ro*
green	*mi-do-ri*
grey	*ha-i-i-ro*

orange	*o-ren-ji-i-ro*
pearl white	*shin-ju-i-ro*
pink	*pin-ku*
purple	*mu-ra-sa-ki*
red	*a-ka*
silver	*gin-i-ro*
sky blue	*so-ra-i-ro*
violet	*su-mi-re-i-ro*
white	*shi-ro*
yellow	*ki-i-ro*

PARTS OF THE BODY...*ka-ra-da*

arm	*u-de*
armpit	*wa-ki*
back	*se-na-ka*
belly	*ha-ra*
blood	*chi*
cheek	*ho-o*
chest	*mu-ne*
chin	*a-go*
dimple	*e-ku-bo*
ear	*mi-mi*
elbow	*hi-ji*
esophagus	*sho-ku-do*
eye	*me*

173

eyebrow	*ma-yu-ge*
eye lash	*ma-tsu-ge*
face	*ka-o*
false teeth	*i-re-ba*
finger	*yu-bi*
foot	*a-shi*
forehead	*hi-ta-i*
hair	*ka-mi*
hand	*te*
head	*a-ta-ma*
heart	*shin-zō*
heel	*ka-ka-to*
hip	*ko-shi*
jaw	*a-go*
kidney	*jin-zō*
knee	*hi-za*
leg	*a-shi*
lip	*ku-chi-bi-ru*
liver	*kan-zō*
lung	*ha-i*
mouth	*ku-chi*
mustache	*ku-chi-hi-ge*
nail	*tsu-me*
neck	*ku-bi*
nose	*ha-na*
palm	*te-no-hi-ra*
shin	*su-ne*
shoulder	*ka-ta*

stomach	*i*
teeth	*ha*
thigh	*mo-mo*
throat	*no-do*
thumb	*o-ya-yu-bi*
toe	*tsu-ma-sa-ki*
tongue	*shi-ta*
waist	*dō*
wrist	*te-ku-bi*

SPORTS ....*un-dō*

auto race	*ji-dō-sha rē-su*
badminton	*ba-do-min-ton*
baseball	*ya-kyū*
basketball	*ba-su-ket-to*
bowling	*bō-rin-gu*
boxing	*bo-ku-shin-gu*
cycling	*sa-i-ku-rin-gu*
diving	*da-i-bin-gu; to-bi-ko-mi*
fencing	*fen-shin-gu*
Japanese fencing	*ken-dō*
football	*fut-to bō-ru, sak-kā*
gliding	*gu-ra-i-dā*
golf	*go-ru-fu*
gymnastics	*ta-i-sō*
horse racing	*ke-i-ba*

175

horseback riding	*jō-ba*
hockey	*hok-kē*
hunting	*han-tin-gu*
ice-hockey	*a-i-su hok-kē*
marathon race	*ma-ra-son*
mountaineering	*to-zan*
rowing	*bō-to*
rugby	*ra-gu-bi-i*
shooting	*sha-ge-ki*
skating	*su-kē-to*
skiing	*su-ki-i*
swimming	*su-i-e-i*
table tennis	*pin-pon*
tennis	*te-ni-su*
track and field	*ri-ku-jō kyō-gi*
water polo	*su-i-kyū*
weight-lifting	*jū-ryō-a-ge*
wrestling	*re-su-rin-gu*
Japanese wrestling	*su-mō*
yachting	*yot-to*

HOUSING ....*su-ma-i*

alcove	*to-ko no ma*
ash tray	*ha-i-za-ra*
basement	*chi-ka-shi-tsu*

176

VOCABULARY

bathroom	*fu-ro-ba*
bedroom	*shin-shi-tsu*
bookcase	*hon-da-na*
carpet	*jū-tan*
ceiling	*ten-jō*
chair	*i-su*
chimney	*en-to-tsu*
curtain	*kā-ten*
cushion	*kus-shon; za-bu-ton*
desk	*tsu-ku-e*
door	*do-a*
downstairs	*ka-i-ka; shi-ta*
electric fan	*sen-pū-ki*
entrance	*gen-kan*
fan	*sen-su*
fence	*he-i*
floor	*yu-ka*
garage	*ga-rē-ji*
garden	*ni-wa*
gate	*mon*
gutter	*to-i*
hedge	*ka-ki-ne*
house	*i-e*
key	*ka-gi*
kitchen	*da-i-do-ko-ro; kit-chin*
living room	*i-ma*
mirror	*ka-ga-mi*
pan	*na-be*

radio	*ra-ji-o*
refrigerator	*re-i-zō-ko*
roof	*ya-ne*
room	*he-ya*
screen	*byō-bu*
shelf	*ta-na*
sofa	*so-fā*
staircase	*ka-i-dan*
straw mat	*ta-ta-mi*
table	*tē-bu-ru*
telephone	*den-wa*
television	*te-re-bi*
terrace	*te-ra-su*
upstairs	*ni-ka-i; u-e*
vacuum cleaner	*den-ki sō-ji-ki*
vase	*ka-bin*
wall	*ka-be*
window	*ma-do*

CLOTHING ....*i-ru-i*

apron	*e-pu-ron*
belt	*be-ru-to; ban-do*
blouse	*bu-ra-u-su*
button	*bo-tan*
cap	*bō-shi*

collar	*ka-rā; e-ri*
comb	*ku-shi*
cotton	*mo-men*
dress	*wan-pi-i-su*
Japanese dress	*ki-mo-no*
glasses	*me-ga-ne*
glove	*te-bu-ku-ro*
handbag	*han-do bag-gu*
hat	*bō-shi*
jacket	*u-wa-gi*
jewelry	*hō-se-ki*
muffler	*ma-fu-rā*
necklace	*nek-ku-re-su*
necktie	*ne-ku-ta-i*
overcoat	*ga-i-tō; kō-to*
pillow	*ma-ku-ra*
pocket	*po-ket-to*
purse	*sa-i-fu*
ring	*yu-bi-wa*
sash	*o-bi*
shawl	*shō-ru*
shoes	*ku-tsu*
silk	*ki-nu*
skirt	*su-kā-to*
sleeve	*so-de*
socks	*ku-tsu-shi-ta*
sport shirt	*su-pō-tsu sha-tsu*
stockings	*ku-tsu-shi-ta*

suit	*se-bi-ro* (men)
	sū-tsu (women)
sweater	*sē-tā*
trousers	*zu-bon*
umbrella	*ka-sa*
underwear	*sha-tsu; shi-ta-gi*
vest	*chok-ki*
white shirt	*wa-i-sha-tsu*
wool	*ū-ru*
wrist watch	*u-de-do-ke-i*

PROFESSIONS ...*sho-ku-gyō*

accountant	*ka-i-ke-i-shi*
actor	*ha-i-yū*
actress	*jo-yū*
advertising agent	*kō-ko-ku gyō*
air force	*kū-gun*
architect	*ken-chi-ku-ka*
army	*ri-ku-gun*
artist	*ge-i-ju-tsu ka*
banker	*gin-kō-ka*
barber	*to-ko-ya*
book seller	*hon-ya*
businessman	*ji-tsu-gyō ka*
business manager	*sō-mu-bu-chō*

butcher	*ni-ku-ya*
carpenter	*da-i-ku*
clerk	*ji-mu-in*
clergyman	*bo-ku-shi*
company employee	*ka-i-sha-in*
conductor	*sha-shō*
(train, etc)	
dentist	*ha-i-sha*
designer	*de-za-i-nā*
diplomat	*ga-i-kō-kan*
director	*jū-ya-ku*
doctor	*i-sha*
dressmaker	*yō-sa-i-ten*
driver	*do-ra-i-bā; un-ten-shu*
electrician	*den-ki-ya*
engineer	*gi-shi, gi-ju-tsu-sha*
florist	*ha-na-ya*
gardener	*u-e-ki-ya ; ni-wa-shi*
general manager	*sō-shi-ha-i-nin*
government official	*ya-ku-nin*
greengrocer	*ya-o-ya*
housewife	*shu-fu*
interpreter	*tsū-ya-ku*
journalist	*jā-na-ri-su-to*
laundryman	*sen-ta-ku-ya*
lawyer	*ben-go-shi*
manager	*shi-ha-i-nin*
managing director	*sen-mu*

military serviceman	*gun-jin*
missionary	*sen-kyō-shi*
musician	*on-ga-ku-ka*
navy	*ka-i-gun*
novelist	*shō-se-tsu ka*
officer	*shō-kō*
orchestra conductor	*shi-ki-sha*
painter	*ga-ka*
photographer	*sha-shin-ka*
physician	*i-sha*
pilot	*pa-i-rot-to*
poet	*shi-jin*
president	*sha-chō; sō-sai*
printer	*in-sa-tsu-ya*
professor	*kyō-ju*
publisher	*shup-pan-sha*
reporter	*shin-bun ki-sha*
retail shop	*ko-u-ri-ten*
sales manager	*e-i-gyō-bu-chō*
salesman	*sē-ru-su man*
scholar	*ga-ku-sha*
sculptor	*chō-ko-ku-ka*
secretary	*hi-sho*
stenotypist	*su-te-no*
student	*ga-ku-sei; se-i-to*
tailor	*yō-fu-ku-ya; tē-rā*
teacher	*sen-se-i*
typist	*ta-i-pi-su-to*

| vice president | *fu-ku-sha-chō* |
| wholesaler | *to-ri-tsu-gi; ton-ya* |

USEFUL ADJECTIVES

active	*ka-tsu-dō te-ki (na)*
amusing	*o-mo-shi-ro-i*
bad	*wa-ru-i*
beautiful	*ki-re-i (na)*
best	*i-chi-ban-yo-i*
big	*ō-ki-i*
bitter	*ni-ga-i*
black	*ku-ro-i*
blue	*a-o-i*
bold	*zū-zū-shi-i; da-i-tan(na)*
brief	*mi-ji-ka-i*
bright	*a-ka-ru-i*
broad	*hi-ro-i*
busy	*i-so-ga-shi-i*
careful	*chū-i bu-ka-i; shin-chō*
careless	*fu-chū-i (na)*
cheap	*ya-su-i*
chilly	*sa-mu-i*
clever	*ka-shi-ko-i*
cold	*tsu-me-ta-i; sa-mu-i*
cool	*su-zu-shi-i*
cunning	*zu-ru-i*

cute	*ka-wa-i-i*
dangerous	*ki-ken (na); a-bu-na-i*
deep	*fu-ka-i*
delicious	*o-i-shi-i*
different	*chi-gat-ta*
difficult	*mu-zu-ka-shi-i*
diligent	*kin-ben (na)*
direct	*cho-ku-se-tsu (no)*
dirty	*ki-ta-na-i*
dishonest	*fu-shō-ji-ki (na)*
easy	*ya-sa-shi-i*
enough	*jū-bun (ni)*
extra	*yo-ke-i (na); rin-ji (no)*
false	*u-so (no)*
far	*tō-i*
fast	*ha-ya-i*
foolish	*ba-ka (na)*
gentle	*ya-sa-shi-i*
good	*yo-i*
gradually	*dan-dan*
great	*i-da-i (na)*
happy	*kō-fu-ku (na)*
hard	*ka-ta-i*
harmful	*yū-ga-i (na)*
heavy (weight)	*o-mo-i*
high (expensive)	*ta-ka-i*
honest	*shō-ji-ki (na)*
idle	*ta-i-da (na)*

important	*ta-i-se-tsu (na)*
interesting	*o-mo-shi-ro-i*
kind	*shin-se-tsu (na)*
large	*ō-ki-i*
late	*o-so-i*
light (weight)	*ka-ru-i*
little	*chi-i-sa-i*
long	*na-ga-i*
lovely	*ka-wa-i-i*
low	*hi-ku-i*
narrow	*se-ma-i*
near	*chi-ka-i*
next	*tsu-gi (no)*
noisy	*u-ru-sa-i*
old (age)	*to-shi-tot-ta*
old	*fu-ru-i*
painful	*i-ta-i*
past	*ka-ko (no)*
patient	*ga-man-zu-yo-i*
peculiar	*hen-na*
pleasant	*ta-no-shi-i*
poor (needy)	*bin-bō (na)*
poor (pitiful)	*ka-wa-i-sō (na)*
present	*i-ma (no)*
pretty	*ki-re-i (na)*
quiet	*shi-zu-ka (na)*
rich	*o-ka-ne-mo-chi (no);*
	yū-fu-ku (na)

sad	*ka-na-shi-i*
same	*o-na-ji*
second hand	*chū-bu-ru (no), chū-ko*
short	*mi-ji-ka-i*
simple	*tan-jun (na)*
skillful	*ki-yō (na)*
slow	*o-so-i*
sly	*zu-ru-i*
small	*chi-i-sa-i*
smelly	*ku-sa-i*
soft	*ya-wa-ra-ka-i*
sour	*sup-pa-i*
straight	*mas-su-gu (na)*
strong	*tsu-yo-i*
such	*kon-na*
sudden	*kyū (na)*
sweet	*a-ma-i*
that	*a-no*
thick	*a-tsu-i*
this	*ko-no*
true	*hon-to (no)*
ugly	*mi-ni-ku-i*
unhappy	*fu-kō (na)*
unusual	*me-zu-ra-shi-i*
various	*i-ro-i-ro (no)*
warm	*a-ta-ta-ka-i*
weak	*yo-wa-i*
white	*shi-ro-i*

wide	*hi-ro-i*
wise	*ka-shi-ko-i*
wonderful	*su-ba-ra-shi-i*
young	*wa-ka-i*

USEFUL VERBS

advertise	*kō-ko-ku-su-ru*
answer	*ko-ta-e-ru*
apologize	*a-ya-ma-ru*
arrive	*tsu-ku*
begin	*ha-ji-ma-ru*
believe	*shin-zu-ru*
bite	*ka-mu*
boil	*ni-ru*
borrow	*ka-ri-ru*
break	*ko-wa-su*
bring	*mot-te-ku-ru*
build	*ta-te-ru*
burn	*ya-ku*
buy	*ka-u*
catch	*tsu-ka-ma-e-ru*
change	*ka-e-ru*
cheat	*da-ma-su*
chew	*ka-mu*
choose	*e-ra-bu*
climb	*no-bo-ru*

collect	*a-tsu-me-ru*
come	*ku-ru*
compare	*ku-ra-be-ru*
cook	*ryō-ri-su-ru*
cough	*se-ki-su-ru*
count	*ka-zo-e-ru*
cry	*na-ku*
cut	*ki-ru*
decide	*ki-me-ru*
deliver	*to-do-ke-ru*
deposit	*a-zu-ke-ru*
desire	*no-zo-mu*
die	*shi-nu*
dig	*ho-ru*
discover	*hak-ken-su-ru*
do	*su-ru*
doubt	*u-ta-ga-u*
dream	*yu-me-mi-ru*
drink	*no-mu*
drop	*o-to-su*
dry	*ka-wa-ka-su*
eat	*ta-be-ru*
employ	*ya-to-u*
enjoy	*ta-no-shi-mu*
enter	*ha-i-ru*
exchange	*to-ri-ka-e-ru*
explain	*se-tsu-me-i-su-ru*
feel	*kan-ji-ru*

fight	*ta-ta-ka-u*
find	*mi-tsu-ke-ru*
finish	*su-ma-su, o-e-ru*
fly	*to-bu*
forget	*wa-su-re-ru*
forgive	*yu-ru-su*
freeze	*kō-ru*
gather	*a-tsu-me-ru*
give	*a-ge-ru*
go	*i-ku*
greet	*a-i-sa-tsu-su-ru*
guess	*a-te-ru*
guide	*an-na-i-su-ru*
hang	*ka-ke-ru*
hate	*ki-ra-u*
have	*mo-tsu*
hear	*ki-ku*
help	*ta-su-ke-ru*
hide	*ka-ku-su*
hold	*mo-tsu*
hope	*no-zo-mu*
hurry	*i-so-gu*
injure	*i-ta-me-ru*
instruct	*o-shi-e-ru*
introduce	*shō-ka-i-su-ru*
invent	*ha-tsu-me-i-su-ru*
invite	*shō-ta-i-su-ru*
jump	*to-bu*

kick	*ke-ru*
kill	*ko-ro-su*
know	*shi-ru*
laugh	*wa-ra-u*
learn	*na-ra-u*
lend	*ka-su*
like	*su-ku*
listen	*ki-ku*
live	*su-mu*
look	*mi-ru*
love	*a-i-su-ru*
make	*tsu-ku-ru*
measure	*ha-ka-ru*
meet	*a-u*
melt	*to-ke-ru*
miss	*u-shi-na-u*
mix	*ma-ze-ru*
move	*u-go-ku*
notify	*shi-ra-se-ru*
obey	*shi-ta-ga-u*
open	*a-ke-ru*
oppose	*han-ta-i-su-ru*
order	*chū-mon-su-ru*
pay	*ha-ra-u*
play	*a-so-bu*
postpone	*no-ba-su*
pray	*i-no-ru*
print	*in-sa-tsu-su-ru*

push	*o-su*
reach	*tsu-ku*
read	*yo-mu*
refuse	*ko-to-wa-ru*
repeat	*ku-ri-ka-e-su*
reply	*ko-ta-e-ru*
request	*yō-kyū-su-ru*
return	*ka-e-ru*
ride	*no-ru*
run	*ha-shi-ru*
see	*mi-ru*
sell	*u-ru*
send	*o-ku-ru*
sew	*nu-u*
show	*mi-se-ru*
sing	*u-ta-u*
sink	*shi-zu-mu*
sit	*su-wa-ru*
sleep	*ne-ru*
speak	*ha-na-su*
stand	*ta-tsu*
steal	*nu-su-mu*
stop	*to-me-ru*
study	*ben-kyō-su-ru*
surprise	*o-do-ro-ku*
sweep	*ha-ku*
swim	*o-yo-gu*
talk	*ha-na-su*

teach	*o-shi-e-ru*
tell	*tsu-ge-ru*
think	*o-mo-u*
throw	*na-ge-ru*
tie	*mu-su-bu*
touch	*sa-wa-ru*
translate	*hon-ya-ku-su-ru*
travel	*ryo-kō-su-ru*
try	*ta-me-su*
understand	*wa-ka-ru*
use	*tsu-ka-u*
visit	*hō-mon-su-ru*
wait	*ma-tsu*
wake	*o-ki-ru*
wash	*a-ra-u*
wear	*ki-ru*
weep	*na-ku*
weigh	*ha-ka-ru*
wipe	*fu-ku*
wish	*ne-ga-u*
work	*ha-ta-ra-ku*
worry	*shin-pa-i-su-ru*
wrap	*tsu-tsu-mu*
write	*ka-ku*